CENTRAL LONDON

PAST AND PRESENT

Volume 2

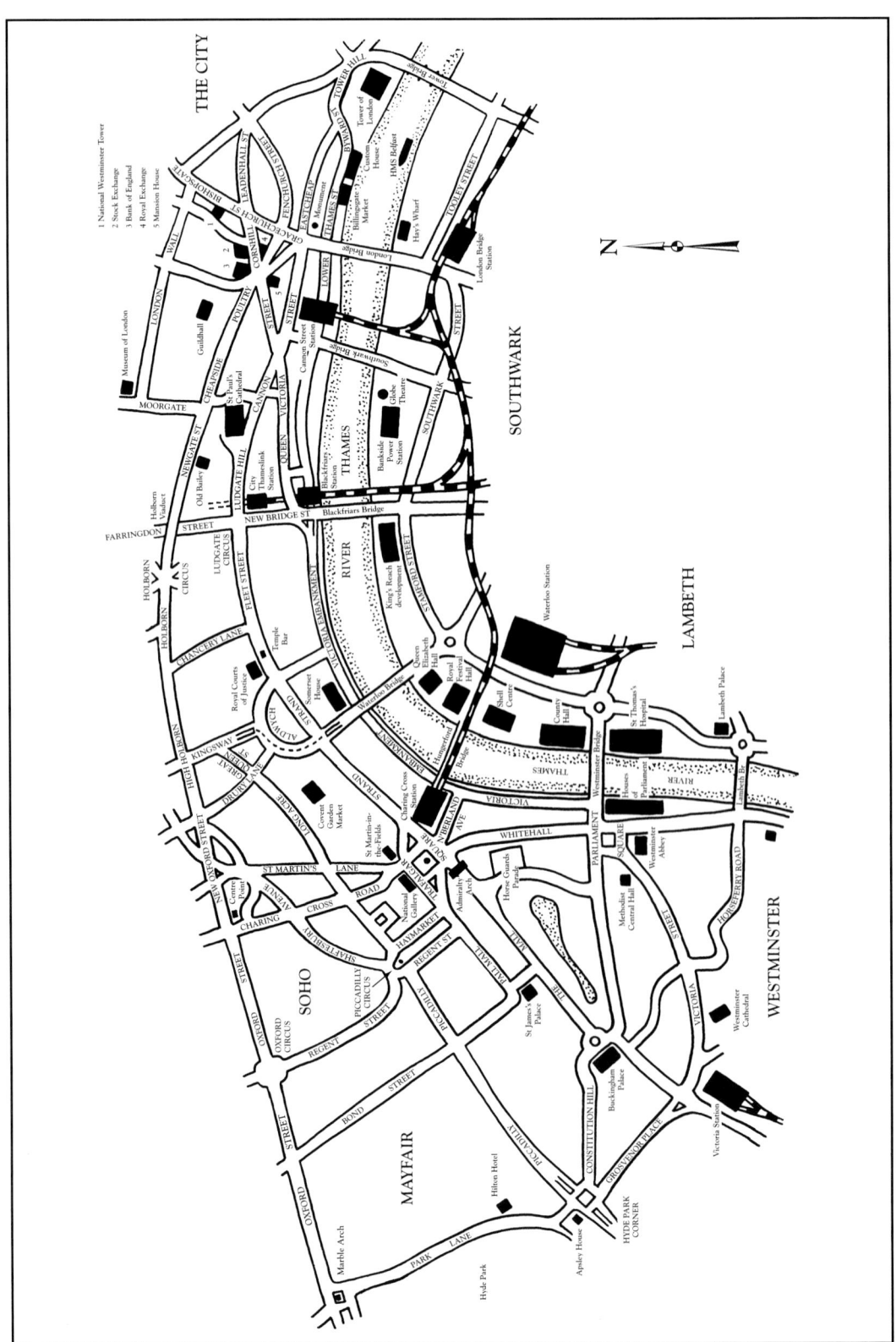

Central London: the area covered by this book is west and south of Charing Cross Road and Hungerford Bridge, while its companion volume *South Bank and the City* deals with the area east and north of that line.

CENTRAL LONDON
PAST AND PRESENT

Volume 2
WESTMINSTER AND THE WEST END

Will & Tricia Adams

·THE HERITAGE OF BRITAIN·
from
The NOSTALGIA Collection

© Past & Present Publishing Ltd 1997 and 2003

All rights reserved. No part of this publication may be reproduced, stored in a retrieval system or transmitted, in any form or by any means, electronic, mechanical, photocopying, recording or otherwise, without prior permission in writing from Past & Present Publishing Ltd.

First published in 1997 as part of London: A nostalgic look at the capital since 1945
Updated two-volume paperback edition first published in 2003

British Library Cataloguing in Publication Data

A catalogue record for this book is available from the British Library.

ISBN 1 85895 151 8

Past & Present Publishing Ltd
The Trundle
Ringstead Road
Great Addington
Kettering
Northants NN14 4BW

Tel/Fax: 01536 330588
email: sales@nostalgiacollection.com
Website: www.nostalgiacollection.com

Printed and bound in Great Britain

A Past & Present book
from
The **NOSTALGIA** *Collection*

ACKNOWLEDGEMENTS

Someone once wrote that if you steal from one author, it's plagiarism; if you steal from many, it's research. Well, a good deal of 'theft' has occurred in the research from this book, and while the principal titles consulted are listed below, we would like in particular to express our gratitude for the scholarship of Ben Weinreb and Christopher Hibbert, Editors of The London Encyclopaedia (published by Macmillan). This is without doubt the essential reference book on London, its 1,060 pages crammed with more comprehensive yet readable information on the capital than any other available. Anyone with more than a passing interest in London's history *must* have a copy. The other indispensable handbook that we always carried with us was Nicholas Pevsner and Bridget Cherry's The Buildings of England: London, Volumes 1 and 2 (published by Penguin), covering London north and south of the Thames respectively. Again, the essential scholarship is leavened by an acerbic architectural criticism that is pure joy. Don't set off through London on foot without it!

We would also like to express our gratitude to the contributors of the 'past' photographs. We were very fortunate to be able to obtain most of the views from just a few private sources: Neil Davenport and his late father, Arthur Davenport; Frank Hornby and, through him, N. L. Browne and A. J. Pike; and Allan Mott, who allowed us access to the C. F. B. Penley collection and that of his late father, Charles Mott. The other important source was the excellent Photo Library of the London Transport Museum, Covent Garden, and we would like to thank Sheila Taylor and Jane Ramsay for their valued assistance. The other photographers are credited individually, and we are most grateful for their keen interest in and help with this project.

Many other people helped in many ways with the preparation of this book, and we would like to express our thanks to John Broughton, for developing and printing the 'present' views so expertly; Colin Whyman, for arranging access to the top of the Shell Tower to take the required 'present' views, and Shell for granting the facility; John Day at the Department of Transport for furnishing traffic statistics; Natasha at Guinness Archives; Prudential Assurance at Minster Court; Sally Mason and Richard Belcham at the South Bank Centre; and the library staff of Westminster City Archives.

CONTENTS

Introduction	7
Thames panorama	9
Trafalgar Square and Piccadilly Circus	25
Royal London	41
Westminster	52
Victoria panorama	65
The West End	76
Index	96

BIBLIOGRAPHY

Barker, Felix, and Jackson, Peter *London: 2000 years of a city and its people* (Cassell Ltd, 1974)

Cameron, Robert, and Cooke, Alistair *Above London* (The Bodley Head, 1980)

Day, John R. *London's Trams and Trolleybuses* (London Transport, 1977)

Halliwell, Leslie, with Purser, Philip *Halliwell's Television Companion*, 2nd edition (Paladin, 1985)

Hilditch, Neville (compiled by) *In Praise of London* (Frederick Muller Ltd, 1944)

Guide to London, 54th edition (Ward, Lock & Co, c1940)

Jackson, Alan A. *London's Termini* (David & Charles, 1969)

Jackson, Alan A., and Croome, Desmond F. *Rails Through the Clay: a history of London's tube railways* (George Allen & Unwin, 1962)

Jones, Edward, and Woodward, Christopher *A Guide to the Architecture of London* (Weidenfeld & Nicolson, 1983)

Kent, William (edited by) *An Encyclopaedia of London* (J. M. Dent & Sons Ltd, 1937)

Mee, Arthur *The King's England: London*, 6th impression (Hodder & Stoughton, 1951)

Middleditch, Michael *The Penguin London Mapguide* (Penguin Books, 1994)

Nicholson, Louise *London: Louise Nicholson's Definitive Guide* (revised edition, The Bodley head, 1990)

Pevsner, Nikolaus, and Cherry, Bridget *The Buildings of England: London*, Volume 1, 3rd edition (Penguin Books, 1973)
Volume 2 (Penguin Books, 1983)

Reed, John *RT Jubilee: fifty years of a classic London bus* (Silver Link Publishing Ltd, 1989)

Walker, John (edited by) *Halliwell's Filmgoer's Companion*, 10th edition (HarperCollins, 1993)
Halliwell's Film Guide, 8th edition (Grafton, 1992)

Weinreb, Ben, and Hibbert, Christopher (edited by) *The London Encyclopaedia*, revised edition (Macmillan Reference Books, 1995)

London past and present: 1,800 years in 50 yards! Some appreciation of the vast span of London's history can be gained from this view across Queen Victoria Street in the City. In the foreground are the remains of the 2nd-century AD Temple of Mithras, the god of light and the sun of the ancient Persians, whose name means 'friend'. Long buried beneath the layers of later centuries, in 1889 part of a sculpture hinting at its existence was found buried in the nearby Walbrook, one of the streams beside which the infant city grew. Then bomb damage in the Second World War enabled excavation of the site in the 1950s prior to redevelopment. Across Queen Victoria Street, cut diagonally through the City in 1867-71 (with the District Line running beneath it), is the controversial No 1 Poultry, property developer Lord Palumbo's long-fought-for development overlooking the very heart of the City at Bank. Like it or loathe it ('the most savage blow to the City's heritage since the Luftwaffe' – Save Britain's Heritage), there is no more potent symbol of 21st-century London, representing a new kind of temple to a very different god – Commerce! WA

INTRODUCTION

In the Introduction to the companion volume, *South Bank and the City*, we gave some explanation and justification for the post-war time-scale of these 'past and present' comparisons, perhaps the main one being the element of 'nostalgia', keeping the contrasts firmly within living memory. Through the medium of pairs of photographs separated only in time, we can juxtapose a moment caught on film in, say, 1956 with one captured in exactly the same place four decades later, providing us with that leap back into the recent past, a powerful reminder of all those little details of daily life that we were not even aware that we had forgotten.

Of course this makes it a principally visual, pictorial exercise, but during the research for the captions we came upon many instances of fascinating *written* nostalgia, in particular in period guide books, which served to highlight once again the vast changes that have taken place to every aspect of our apparently staid, humdrum daily lives since the 1940s.

Perhaps the most obvious is the growth of vehicular traffic, motor car use having grown to become an all-invasive and alienating influence. Traffic congestion and pollution is nothing new to London, of course – the conglomerations of horse-drawn buses and wagons jamming every central street in Victorian and Edwardian photographs demonstrate that. But then the streets were also teeming with people dodging the noisy, malodorous but walking-pace congestion. Increasingly during the period under review the pedestrian, as in every other large city, has been corralled on the pavements by railings, allowed out into traffic-land only when the 'green man' allows it, or banished to unnatural elevated walkways or burrowing subways. Pedestrianisation is an increasingly popular and successful solution, but it is still an unnatural environment forced on us by vehicles that we have created and encouraged, but which are now considered too dangerous for us to be allowed to mingle with. Even the increasingly prevalent bicycle, probably the capital's fastest-moving vehicle, poses a threat to the pedestrian worse than the walking dray-horse of yesteryear!

That is not to say that the motor car holds total sway, which is certainly not the case, as anyone who has tried to drive round London recently will confirm. Draconian traffic management is strictly applied. One-way streets, restricted access, yellow lines, parking meters and traffic wardens have all been part of the London scene for 40 years or more.

Ward Lock's *Red Guide* to London of 1940 offers the following advice: 'Only drivers of nerve and experience should motor in the crowded thoroughfares of London... It should be borne in mind that certain **one-way thoroughfares** are closed to all vehicular traffic except that proceeding in a prescribed direction; and that at certain busy spots ... the gyratory or **"roundabout" system** of traffic control is observed: instead of cutting through crossing traffic one turns left and follows the "circus" until the desired turning is reached. By this means much annoying delay is obviated... [The] congested state of the streets robs motoring of any pleasure, while the Underground is generally much quicker.

'Owing to traffic congestion the rules regarding car-parking have to be enforced strictly in the busier quarters of London, and before leaving a car standing it is well to consult a policeman concerning the period during which cars may be so left there, if indeed they may be left there at all...'

Fifty years later, Louise Nicholson, in her excellent *Definitive Guide to London*, echoes those sentiments: 'Driving in London during weekdays is best avoided. Most of the time is spent in traffic jams, looking for a parking place or trying to master the one-way system to reach a car park. When you give up in desperation and leave the car illegally parked, a parking ticket arrives on the windscreen and a clamp on the wheel... Better by far invest in a London travel pass.' Plus ça change...

Another marked change evident in many of the photographs is the matter of dress. In 1940 visitors 'desirous of doing in London as Londoners do may welcome a hint or two under this head, though great latitude is allowed, and all varieties of costume may be seen in the streets. For formal calls and social events of importance a black morning coat and silk hat are *de rigueur*, but City and business men are content with lounge suits, and soft felt hats and "bowlers" are generally worn. Evening dress is usual when dining at high-class restaurants... At theatres, evening dress is nearly always worn in the boxes and stalls, and generally in the dress circle.'

In 1940 Lyons and Slaters were recommended for 'a fair light luncheon for 1s 6d or 2s; a dinner from 2s to 5s; while fare of a lighter kind can be had at the shops of the Aerated Bread Co Ltd, J. Lyons & Co Ltd, Express Dairies Co Ltd, Messrs Fuller, and others... A number of restaurants catering specially for their own "nationals" – the Indian, Spanish, Chinese, etc – are increasingly patronised by British people accustomed to foreign travel or attracted to novel dishes.' Today, of course, American, Chinese and Indian cuisine is second nature; indeed, the traditional British 'meat and two veg', once a restaurant staple, is virtually unknown.

The recent communications revolution leads us to forget the unfamiliarity and rigmarole of making long-distance calls not so long ago. In 1940 'public telephone call office facilities' were provided 'at many post offices, railway stations and shops; and in kiosks. The minimum charge for the use of a call office is 2d. Normally the charge is based upon the radial distance between the exchanges concerned, but details of the charges applicable in London are exhibited in every call office. Trunk (and toll) calls may be effected from practically all public call offices: a call office charge of 2d is payable in addition to the appropriate trunk, etc, charge.

'A message may be dictated from a call office to any post office in the United Kingdom which is a telephone express delivery office for delivery by express messenger, on payment of the appropriate telephone fee for the call (including a call office fee of 2d) plus a writing-down fee of 3d for the first 30 words and 1d for each 10 words or part thereof in excess of 30; plus the express delivery charge of 6d a mile, or part of a mile, from the office of delivery to the addressee.' Phew – thank heavens for today's fax and 'texting' on the 'mobile'!

For the tourist, getting to grips with money has also always been important, and this too has changed completely since the war. 'Gold coins (sovereigns and half-sovereigns) have practically disappeared,' says the *Red Guide*, 'being replaced by **Treasury Notes** of the face value of 20 shillings (green) and ten shillings (brown and slightly smaller). The silver coins are the crown (5s), now very rare; half crown (2s 6d); florin (2s); shilling; sixpence (half a shilling); and "threepenny bits". Be careful to distinguish between half-crowns and florins; the former are larger. Bronze or copper: penny (1d), halfpenny (½d), and farthing (¼d). Farthings are but little used except at draper's establishments and in the poorer districts. Notes are also issued by the Bank of England for sums of £5, £10, £20, £50 and upwards.'

Some readers will become misty-eyed at the nostalgic mention of coins like the half-crown and florin, but the combined effects of inflation and decimalisation saw the end of the farthing as early as 1960, and new 5p and 10p coins were introduced in 1968, supplementing and eventually replacing the shilling and florin coins respectively upon full decimalisation in February 1971. Meanwhile, in 1969 a new 50p coin had replaced the 'ten-bob note'. The halfpenny has subsequently been a casualty, the 5p coin redesigned, the 20p coin introduced, and the £1 and £2 coins are a more durable replacement for the bank-note. Even today, more than a quarter of a century after decimalisation, the 'old' (or, to some, 'real') money is remembered with great affection.

Most of the 'present' photographs were taken in late May 1996, and although it is impossible to keep a book such as this entirely up to date, a few 're-shoots' of the more dramatic developments were taken in March 2000.

THAMES PANORAMA

The western extremity of the area covered by this book is **MILLBANK**, seen here from the Albert Embankment on the south bank of the Thames just upstream of Lambeth Bridge. Note the characteristic riverside lamp standard, with the entwined dolphins at its base, one of many modelled for the new Albert and Victoria Embankments in 1870, and reproduced since for new work. Also linking the two views is Millbank Tower, seen in the 'past' view on 21 January 1961 under construction; it was built for the Vickers Group and completed in 1963. With 32 floors and a height of 387 feet, its concave/convex glazed sides give it a much lighter feel than its slightly lower but contemporary rival the Shell Tower.

A little to the left can be seen the domed roof of the Tate Gallery, built in 1897 on the site of Millbank Penitentiary, a prison completed in 1821 when Millbank (where Westminster Abbey's mill stood in the 16th century) was muddy, marshy wasteground. The building on the extreme right, now thoroughly cleaned, is Thames House (1928), containing government offices.
C. F. B. Penley, A. Mott collection/WA

On the 'south' (actually east) bank and immediately downstream of Lambeth Bridge is **LAMBETH PALACE**, which has been the residence of the Archbishops of Canterbury since the 12th century, so it is perhaps not surprising that little has changed in this historic corner of London in the last 40 years! The fine Tudor brick-built gatehouse is known as Morton's Tower; behind it is the Hall, whose great hammerbeam roof had to be restored following wartime damage. To the right is the church of St Mary-at-Lambeth. In olden days, before the Embankment was built, the Palace was approached directly from the river, where Lambeth Pier now stands. Note the naval vessel moored on the right in the September 1956 photograph, while an ice-cream van and tourist coaches are prominent in 1996. *Frank Hornby/WA*

This majestic view of the Houses of Parliament from **LAMBETH BRIDGE** has changed little since the building was finally completed in 1860, except for the cleaning of the stonework bringing its superb Gothic lines into sharper relief. The other subtle difference between the two views is the state of the tide. Twice a day the Thames rises and falls over 7 metres in the vicinity of the anti-flood barrier across the river at Woolwich, and even this far upstream the difference can be clearly seen when one looks at the supports for Lambeth Pier and the piers of Westminster Bridge in the background. The building on the pier seems to have been replaced by a larger one since the 'past' picture was taken on 24 September 1955.

The river is also, of course, much cleaner than it was, even in recent years. During the hot summer of 1858 came 'the Great Stink'; the Speaker of the House of Commons said, 'They had built ... a magnificent palace for the legislature, but how could they direct the attention of any foreigner to it, when he would be welcomed by a stench which was overpowering?' River excursions were stopped and Parliament's windows draped with sheets soaked in chloride of lime. In the 1860s better drainage began to improve the situation, and the open sewer that was the Thames is now cleaner than it has been for 200 years; in 1974 a salmon was caught in it, the first since about 1840. The Thames now supports 114 fish species, and heron and cormorant are moving into central London. One cause for concern, though, is that the continual narrowing and constraining of the river between vertical walls (in Roman times it was hundreds of yards wide) is threatening this new habitat and increasing the risk of flooding.

Incidentally, until the first Westminster Bridge was opened in 1750 the only places to cross the Thames were by London Bridge or the horse ferry here at Millbank. The considerable sum of £25,000 compensation was paid to the watermen when Westminster Bridge was built, and several thousand to the Archbishop of Canterbury, who owned the ferry rights. *Frank Hornby/WA*

This Victorian engraving of the original **WESTMINSTER BRIDGE** in 1754 is included to give an impression of what Westminster looked like before the present Palace of Westminster was built (1837-58) after the original buildings were destroyed by fire in 1834. Westminster Hall, the turreted building at the end of the bridge, was the only building to survive the fire, and was incorporated in the new Palace of Westminster.

In the second view, taken from the terrace in front of County Hall some time in the mid-1960s, we look across to Westminster Bridge and the dour, soot-blackened **HOUSES OF PARLIAMENT**, with the roof of Westminster Abbey beyond. In the background the new New Scotland Yard tower is under construction.

The first Westminster Bridge, built of masonry, had opened in 1750; no dogs were allowed and anyone defacing the walls was threatened with death! There were, however, problems with the foundations, and the present cast-iron bridge was constructed in 1854-62; its great width of 84 feet was most unusual at the time.

In 2000 the Houses of Parliament have been cleaned, highlighting the Gothic splendour of the architecture, and the bridge has recently fully re-opened following major strengthening work. The major difference between the two views is on the right, with the new building on the corner of Bridge Street and Victoria Embankment. This is Portcullis House, a parliamentary annex built to house around 200 MPs, and the construction of which paralleled work on the Underground Jubilee Line Extension beneath it (see page 59). Controversy arose in early 1999 when the full cost of the building and its fittings were released; its overall £250 million price tag included £1.3 million just for the members' desks, tables and filing cabinets, and £30 million for the blast-proof bronze cladding. *David Keane/WA*

Looking in the opposite direction from the Victoria Tower Gardens adjacent to the Houses of Parliament on 20 April 1957, we see two of the south bank's earliest notable buildings, **ST THOMAS'S HOSPITAL** and **COUNTY HALL**. St Thomas's, on the right, is of 11th century origin but was named after 12th-century martyr St Thomas à Becket. Queen Victoria laid the foundation stone in 1868 and opened the hospital in 1871. It was built on the 'block' or 'pavilion' principle popular on the Continent and approved by Florence Nightingale (who established her Nightingale Training School of Nursing here and revolutionised the profession). The idea was to allow maximum ventilation and air circulation. There were originally seven pavilions ranged along the 1,666-foot length of the building, each with three wards above a service floor, but following war damage and subsequent demolition at the northern end of the site, only the three southern blocks remain. The hospital's new block, completed in 1976, sits rather awkwardly alongside the Victorian original. Note how the trees have grown along this first section of public promenade to be built on the south bank.

The design of County Hall, on the left, built as the headquarters of the erstwhile London County Council, was put out to competition in 1908; begun in 1912, it was not completed until 1922, construction having been interrupted by the First World War. The river frontage is 700 feet long, with a large concave colonnade in the centre. During the construction a sunken Roman barge was found in the mud, now on display at the London Museum. The LCC became the Greater London Council in 1965, then the GLC was abolished in 1986, leaving London as the only major European capital without an overall controlling authority until the more recent mayoral elections. County Hall was offered for sale, and in 1992 was sold to Japanese millionaire Takashi Shirayama for £60 million, who in turn sold it on a lease to the Whitbread Group for conversion into a hotel. Further controversy was fuelled when the Japanese owner refused to allow ex-servicemen to hold a remembrance service at the building's war memorial. In 1997 The London Aquarium was opened in the basement; it is one of Europe's largest, and London's first, exhibits of live fish and marine life.
Frank Hornby/WA

Rising above County Hall in the 'present' view opposite can clearly be seen the Shell Tower, part of the large complex of buildings on the South Bank between County Hall and Hungerford Bridge, and seen here approaching completion in September 1962. Following completion of the 26-storey, 338-foot tower the following year, the viewing gallery afforded stupendous panoramic views across London. Today building work and security considerations mean that the gallery is completely closed, but we are grateful to Shell for allowing photographer Colin Whyman access to the gallery to take the following sequence of 'present' photographs.
Frank Hornby

One tends to think of the Thames as passing through London from west to east, but this view upstream, seen on 18 May 1963 and June 1996, is actually looking almost due south. In the right foreground is County Hall, its offices set around courtyards faced with white glazed tiles, with the Council Chamber in the centre. A more modern extension of the offices is just being completed on the left in 1963. The large Victorian complex of buildings beyond Westminster Bridge is St Thomas's Hospital. As already mentioned, the north end of the complex was badly bombed during the war, and a broken edge of building can be seen in the 1963 view just above the roof of County Hall, while the new East Wing is seen under construction on the left. In 1969-76 the new north block was built, a white cube contrasting severely with the remaining Victorian buildings.

Thames panorama

In the distance, beyond Lambeth Bridge on the west bank, is Millbank Tower, and in front of it the three 1928 Edwardian-style blocks housing ICI and government offices. In the distance can be seen Battersea Power Station of 1929-35; it chimneys are still smoking in 1963, but it finally closed in 1983.

Two particular contrasts between the two views are the growth of the trees, outside the rear of County Hall and on both sides of the river, and the present-day cleanness of the buildings (including the Houses of Parliament, extreme right). *Frank Hornby/Colin Whyman*

We now swing the camera round towards the south-west to look at Westminster Bridge and the Houses of Parliament, the 'past' picture dating from the late 1960s, with the three 200-foot-high slabs of the Department of the Environment under construction in the left background. Note that both pictures were taken at exactly 2.10pm.

Already the distant area round Victoria is built up with tower blocks, several more having joined them in the following 30 years. The tower of Westminster (RC) Cathedral is right of centre in the distance, and to its right can be seen the nearer domed roof of the Methodist Central Hall. Nearer still, on the corner of Bridge Street and Victoria Embankment, demolition of the block of buildings to accommodate Portcullis House and to aid the construction of the Jubilee Line Extension (see pages 12-3) is perhaps the biggest difference between the two pictures.

At the extreme right, on the Embankment, is New Scotland Yard, familiar as the

headquarters of the Metropolitan Police. Originally the Met's headquarters were in Great Scotland Yard, towards the top of Whitehall next to Trafalgar Square. When these new premises were built in 1890, appropriately built with granite dug by Dartmoor convicts, they were named New Scotland Yard. Then in 1967 a move was made to a third headquarters off Victoria Street, bearing the same name but which perhaps should have been *New New Scotland Yard!* This is the 20-storey block with the black upper floor most clearly seen in the 1960s photograph between Westminster Cathedral and Central Hall. Note again how much cleaner the Houses of Parliament are today, while St Margaret's Church and Westminster Abbey beyond positively gleam in their new-found whiteness! Queen Boadicea on her chariot can just be glimpsed at the west end of Westminster Bridge, above the steps leading down to Westminster Pier with its pleasure and ferry boats. *C. F. B. Penley, A. Mott collection/Colin Whyman*

We are now looking due west, and there is very little difference between these two views, the 'past' one taken on 9 August 1967 and the 'present' nearly 30 years later. For here we are looking over Government London and Royal London, left largely unscathed by the war and still displaying all the architectural pomp and circumstance of the administrative heart of the nation. Note again, though, how virtually every major building in view has been cleaned, losing the unsightly soot-stains of pre-Clean Air Act London.

In the centre of the pictures, on Victoria Embankment, is the Royal Air Force Memorial of 1923, surmounted by its gold eagle. Behind it is the rather severe block of the

Ministry of Defence building, designed in 1913 but only completed in the late 1950s. Its utilitarian walls with their plain windows and strange east-west upper blocks, likened by Pevsner to 'two-storeyed houses … stranded high up', led him to describe the building as a 'monument of tiredness'. Certainly it contrasts unfavourably with the buildings on the right, Whitehall Court of 1884, with all its Victorian exuberance.

Immediately to the left of the Ministry of Defence, and on the far side of Whitehall, is Downing Street, the roofs of which can just be seen. To its left is the square block of the Foreign Office, and above it the frontage of Buckingham Palace at the far end of St James's Park. Diagonally back towards Whitehall runs The Mall, shrouded in trees, bounded at its right-hand end by the white facade of Carlton House Terrace. The tall building in the centre background is the Hilton Hotel. *C. F. B. Penley, A. Mott collection/Colin Whyman*

The view is now rather more to the north-west, the foreground dominated by Hungerford Bridge. The original crossing was a suspension footbridge, built in 1841-5, but this was removed (and the chains used in Bristol's Clifton Suspension Bridge) when the railway bridge was built in 1863 to carry the South Eastern Railway into Charing Cross station. The new bridge used cast-iron cylinders as well as the old bridge's two main red-brick piers, was some 61 feet wide and carried four railway tracks; because Victoria Embankment did not then exist, nothing more than functional engineering was thought necessary. Footpaths were provided on both sides to replace the suspension bridge. In 1887 the bridge was widened by nearly 50 feet on the upstream (left) side, which again can be seen in the photographs. In 1905 the original lofty arched roof of the station collapsed during maintenance work, and was replaced by the ridge-and-furrow roof seen in the 9 August 1967 photo.

The bridge's functional ugliness was to cause controversy. Before the war, Arthur Mee, in *The King's England*, described it as 'the ugliest thing seen on the Thames', a 'foul structure sprawling across the river on something like huge drainpipes'. As early as 1889 a new elegant road bridge was envisaged; the station would be moved to the south bank, allowing widening of the Strand. The railway company was not keen, however, even though the bridge was no longer strong enough to allow more than two tracks to be used

at a time, and then only with lightweight locomotives. During the First World War there were plans to strengthen the bridge with new piers and metal arches, but nothing happened until a Royal Commission in 1926 recommended a double-decker bridge, road above rail. In 1928 a road bridge alone was again the favoured option with a south-bank station, a plan presented to what was by then the Southern Railway as a matter of national importance. All was agreed, but in 1930 Parliament rejected the idea! In 1936 the double-deck idea raised its ugly head once more, but the Second World War effectively killed all discussion, and 'that ugly red-oxide Behemoth which sprawls from the north to the south' remains today, subject to any future plans for the South Bank complex.

Charing Cross station itself has been the subject of dramatic change since 1967. In the late 1980s the value of the air space above the station platforms was realised by the BR Property Board, the result being the massive and rather striking development straddling the platforms today, known as No 1 Embankment Place. Above the Embankment the over-track 1888 signal box has also been lost with automation of the signalling, and the rationalisation of the track layout has enabled lengthening of one of the platforms.

Dominating the skyline are the Post Office (now British Telecom) Tower and Centre Point, while on the river in 1996 work is in progress on the new Charing Cross Pier. *Authors' collection/C. F. B. Penley, A. Mott collection/Colin Whyman*

This is a closer view of **CHARING CROSS PIER**, a regular stopping place for trips up and down the river, at 11.32am on 24 September 1955. Of the buildings prominent in the background, the one on the left is the New Adelphi. The original Adelphi was an ambitious scheme by the architects James, John and Robert Adam ('Adelphi' is Greek for 'brothers'). They leased the land in the 1770s and built the first of London's great riverside compositions – a quay and vaults at river level surmounted by four streets of elegant brick houses. It was not a success and nearly bankrupted the brothers, and was then altered and spoiled in the Victorian era. In 1936 the central portion was demolished and replaced by the building seen here – 'savagely ungraceful', as Pevsner describes it. Since 1955 it seems to have gained a couple of extra storeys, improving its appearance a little. Next door is the bulk of Shell-Mex House (1931), originally the Cecil Hotel facing the Strand, which opened in 1886 as Europe's largest with 800 bedrooms. Pevsner calls it, accurately, 'thoroughly unsubtle'. Beyond is the Savoy Hotel.

The 'present' view shows that an entirely new and larger Embankment Pier has replaced the old in the late 1990s, and that the size and shape of river-boats has evolved somewhat! While the work was carried out a temporary pier was used a little way downstream. *Frank Hornby/WA*

Trafalgar Square and Piccadilly Circus

Villiers Street runs parallel with Charing Cross Station from the Embankment to Trafalgar Square, and the arches beneath the station were home to the **PLAYERS THEATRE**. This had its origins in the Players' Theatre Club founded in 1927, which had various homes in the West End until it moved to the Villiers Street arches (seen here circa 1980), which had formerly housed a music-hall. Back in 1936 Leonard Sachs, co-founder of the Players, had conceived the idea of recreating Victorian music-hall, and it was members of the company that formed the chorus when Sachs and the very popular *The Good Old Days* moved to television via the stage of the City Varieties Theatre, Leeds. However, it was a production of *The Boy Friend* that opened the new theatre in 1953.

The recent building of the new office premises astride the station meant the Players Theatre moving to temporary premises between 1987 and 1990. Today the frontage is totally transformed by the new Coopers & Lybrand building, No 1 Embankment Place, but echoes of the railway arches are seen in the design of the entrance. *C. Mott, A. Mott collection/ WA*

Today access to the Players Theatre is from the passage that runs beneath the station from Villiers Street to Craven Street, and music-hall is once again the order of the day. *WA*

This is the view of the north side of **TRAFALGAR SQUARE** from the steps of St Martin-in-the-Fields. Again, it is one of London's great focal points, conceived by John Nash, with a road entering from the east (Pall Mall East, at the far end of the Square in this picture) and one from the west (Duncannon Street towards the West Strand Improvements at Charing Cross). But nothing came of his plans for the north side, until Charing Cross Road arrived awkwardly in the north-east corner in the 1880s. Where the National Gallery now stands was the King's Stables, and St Martin's Place (foreground) was the narrow lower end of St Martin's Lane, which ran right down to the Strand. However, all these ramshackle buildings were demolished to make way for the new Square in 1830. The sloping site was exploited by having the north side as a terrace, with steps down into the Square. Above was built the National Gallery, founded in 1824 and built here in 1832-8; from its origin in 38 masterpieces purchased for £57,000, it now houses well over 2,000 pictures.

In this splendid 'past' view dated Thursday 10 September 1953, what might be a Wolseley passes in the foreground while a vintage half-cab coach turns into St Martin's Place. A survey before the war found that this was the second busiest spot in London, with 66,000 vehicles passing through in 12 hours. Today traffic and pedestrian management is more sophisticated, and the roads well marked with lanes. On the skyline, to the left, Canada House has acquired a new roof extension (visible now that the older trees have been replaced by new saplings), and in the centre rises New Zealand House. The distant buildings in Pall Mall East are now obscured by the new Sainsbury Gallery, added in 1985-91 (see also page 41).

In the far corner of the Square (hidden by trees and traffic) is a plinth that has stood empty since the Square was laid out, because no one could decide who or what to put on it. Back in the 1930s Arthur Mee wrote: 'The empty pedestal is waiting for a hero: surely it is the very place for the Chief Scout on his horse.' In the 1990s suggestions included Lady Thatcher, Nelson Mandela and footballer Paul Gascoigne. We suppose it depends on one's idea of a hero. In July 1996 a temporary solution was announced: the Royal Society of Artists would place a different contemporary sculpture on the plinth every eight months until a permanent decision was made. In 1997 a further initiative was announced, World Squares for All, launched by Sir Norman (later Lord) Foster. This would see the pedestrianisation of the top of the Square, releasing it from its current state besieged by traffic (including an astonishing 4,000 buses a day!). Watch this space... *C. F. B. Penley, A. Mott collection/WA*

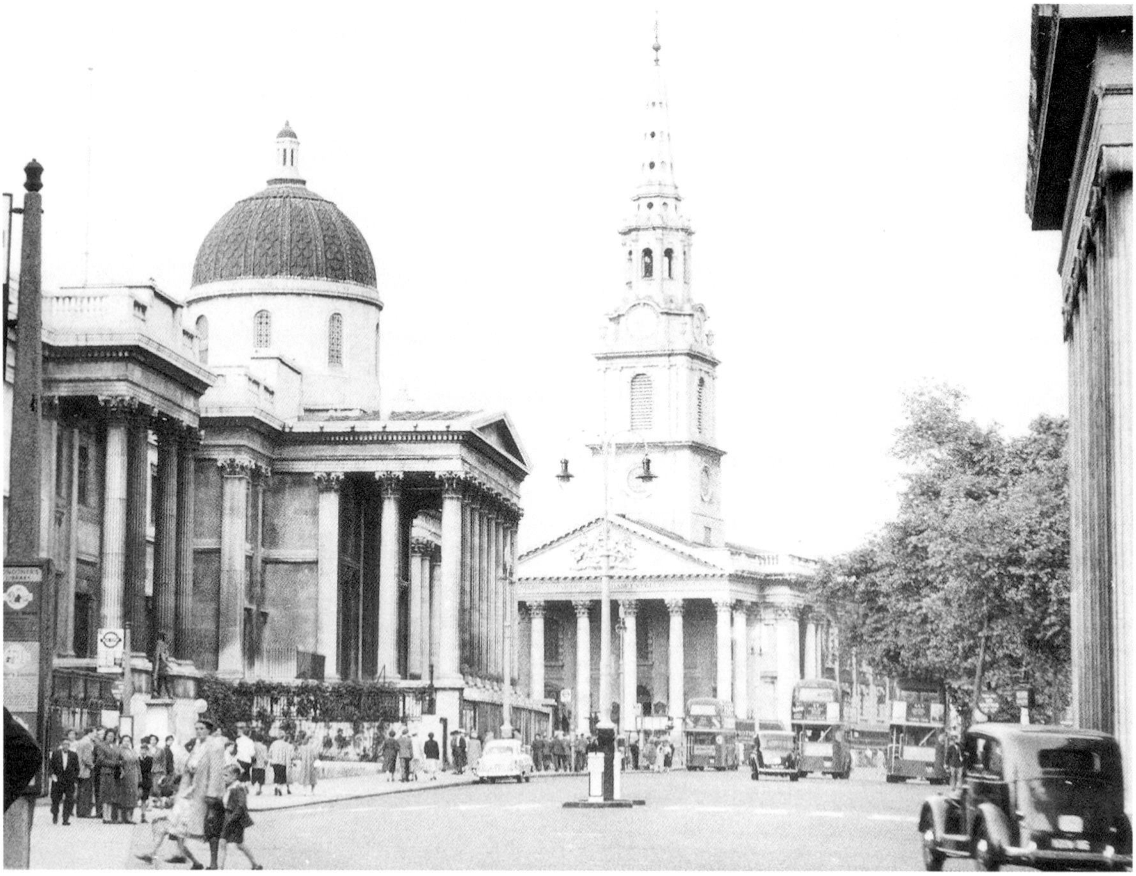

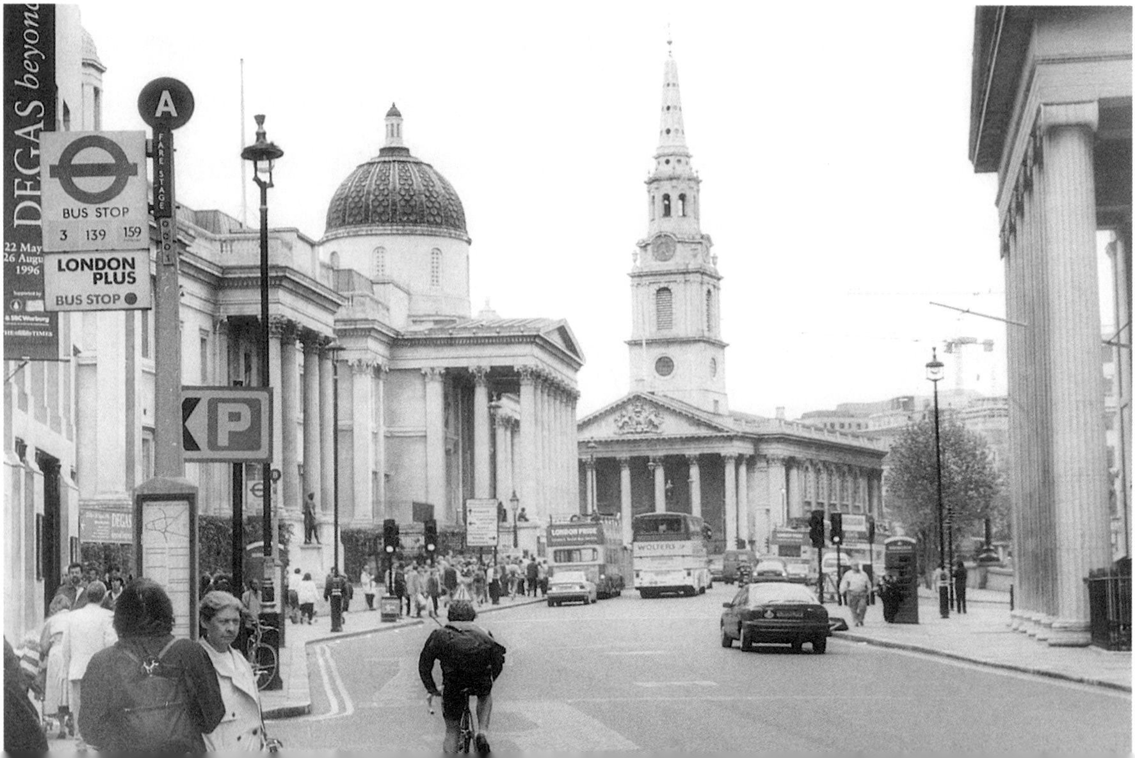
DEGAS beyond
22 May
26 Augu
1996
A
BUS STOP
3 139 159
LONDON PLUS
BUS STOP
FARE STAGE
LONDON PRIDE
WOLTERS

Left We are now looking at the north side of **TRAFALGAR SQUARE** from the other end, in Pall Mall East, the 'past' picture having been taken on Tuesday 22 June 1954. On the left is, of course, the National Gallery, the statue this time being James II, and the background is dominated by St Martin-in-the-Fields. This famous church has its origins in the 13th century, when it would have been very much 'in the fields'! The present building was erected in 1722-6, with its distinctive 'temple front' portico surmounted by a steeple, a design new in England and much copied in America. Buckingham Palace is in its parish, and it has seen many Royal christenings in the past. The crypt was used as a shelter for homeless people after the First World War, and as an air raid shelter during the Second; damaged by bombing, it has since been restored and is used for concerts and meetings, as well as housing the London Brass Rubbing Centre.

On the extreme right in both pictures is the northern portico of Canada House, while the removal of the trees reveals in 1996 the distant cranes atop the Villiers House development in the Strand. Note how the former uncontrolled pedestrian crossing with its central refuge has been replaced by a controlled crossing without a refuge; even though the pavement on the right has been widened considerably, it's an awful long way across when the 'bleeps' are sounding! *C. F. B. Penley, A. Mott collection/WA*

Above Feeding the pigeons in **TRAFALGAR SQUARE** is a traditional London pastime, but it isn't enjoyed by everyone, and there is a certain amount of conflict between the custodians of the Square. The Planning & Environment Committee of Westminster City Council feel that the pigeons should be discouraged – by a ban on feeding and the use of 'birth control' pellets as used elsewhere in Europe – as they are a health risk to children and a cleaning problem for the borough. However, the Square is under the control of the Department of National Heritage, which considers that it should be an exception because of the tradition. Certainly there seem to be fewer pigeons in 1996 than are seen in the 'past' picture taken on 16 January 1965. But birdseed is being sold in vast quantities from both kiosks, in tins in 1965 but now in paper cups. And while the situation was turning Major General Sir Henry Havelock prematurely white in 1965, that seems less of a problem today!

In the left background (hidden by trees in 1996) can be seen the tower of the Coliseum, built in 1904 as a variety theatre; the globe on top used to revolve. It is now London's largest theatre, the first in England to have a revolving stage and the first in Europe to have lifts. In the 1960s it became a cinema, but in 1968 reopened as the new home of the Sadler's Wells Opera Company, which was renamed the English National Opera. On the right is South Africa House of 1935. *Arthur Davenport/WA*

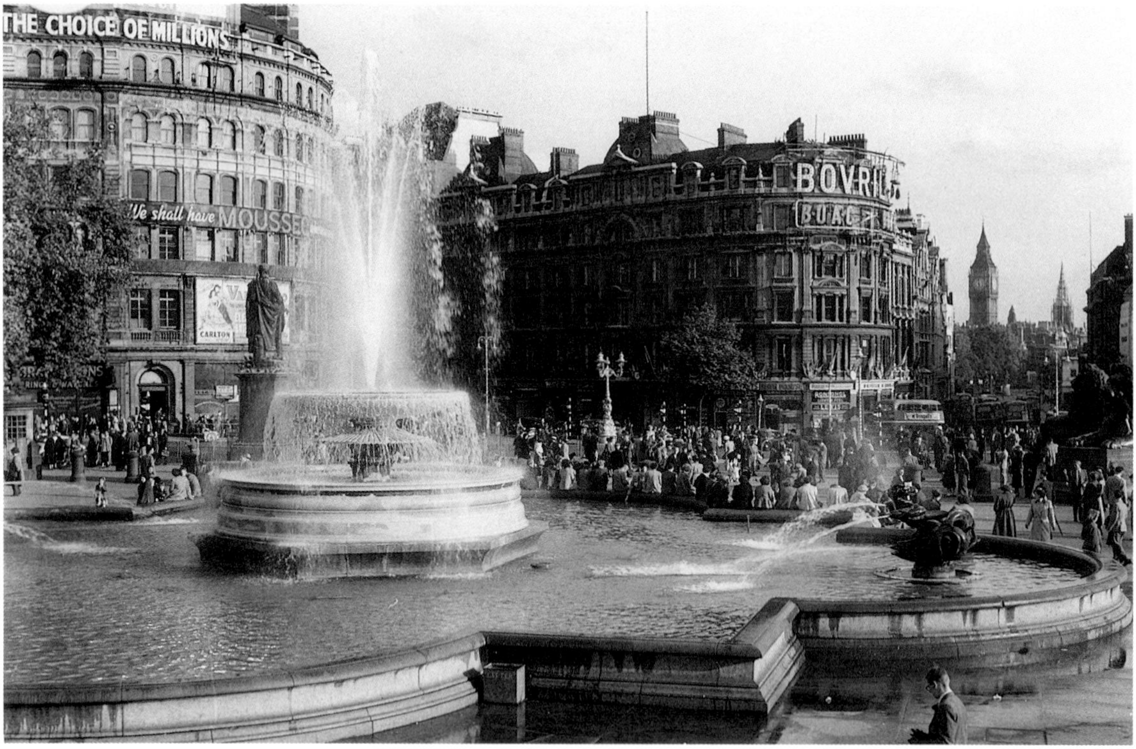
THE CHOICE OF MILLIONS
BOVRIL
CARLTON

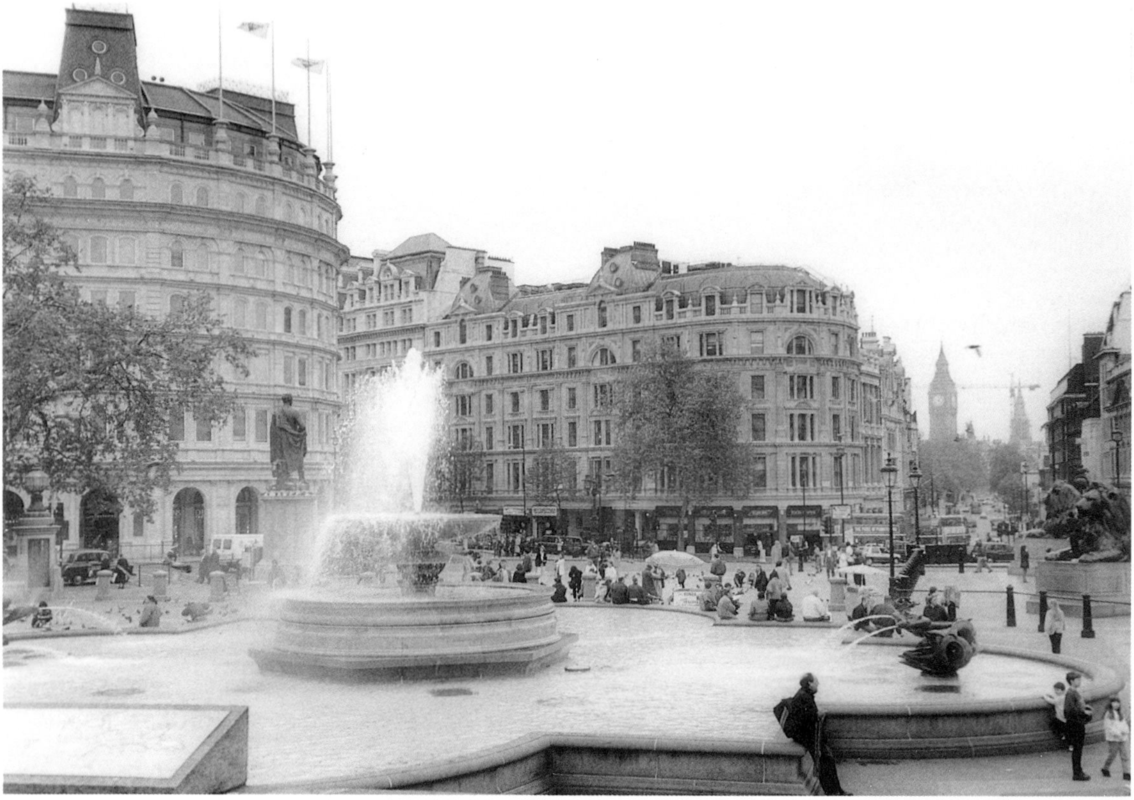

Left 'Here we are at the heart of things,' wrote Arthur Mee of **TRAFALGAR SQUARE** in the 1930s, 'between Piccadilly and the Strand, with Whitehall down to Westminster in front, the National Gallery behind, Canada facing South Africa across the Square…' This is the view from the North Terrace, the past picture taken on Wednesday 29 August 1951. In the foreground is one of the two famous fountains, not part of the original design and only completed in 1845; they were remodelled in 1939, when the mermaids and mermen were added. The south-east corner of the Square seen here used to be occupied by the large square Jacobean London mansion of the Dukes of Northumberland, but this was demolished in 1874 and replaced by Northumberland Avenue and the present buildings. In the 1970s Pevsner described them as 'two big shabby Late Victorian buildings … fussy, commercial, without much dignity or character', but they have been considerably improved in recent years by cleaning and refurbishment, especially that on the left, originally the Grand Hotel. The site was to have been redeveloped, but refurbishment was chosen after a campaign in the *Architects' Journal*. Removal of the advertising hoardings has also helped.

The view down Whitehall (right) towards the Houses of Parliament is impressive, and on the extreme right can be seen two of the four great lions guarding the foot of Nelson's Column; they are 20 feet long and 11 feet high and arrived very late in 1867 (their non-appearance a standing joke in the newspapers of the day), while the column itself, raised in 1839-42, is 170 feet high, surmounted by the 17-foot-high figure of Nelson. *Arthur Davenport/WA*

Right Rising from the south-west corner of Trafalgar Square towards Piccadilly and Piccadilly Circus is **LOWER REGENT STREET**, a continuation of Nash's 'New Street' designed to link Carlton House in Pall Mall with Regent's Park. To avoid cutting into the fashionable St James's area south of Piccadilly, and to allow Regent Street to intersect with the east end of Pall Mall, (upper) Regent Street turned east to enter the side of Piccadilly Circus in front of the County Fire Office (at the top of the street in both of these views), then continued south-eastwards to Waterloo Place in Pall Mall.

Hardly anything has changed in the 43 years separating these two photographs, the 'past' one having been taken at 1.40pm on Saturday 12 September 1953. On the left, with the dome, is the Plaza cinema (today the UCI Plaza), showing the famous Alan Ladd western *Shane*, then on release. In 1996 one of the four Plaza screens is showing the movie version of *Mission Impossible*, which ran on TV from 1966 to 1972. It stars Tom Cruise, who was two years old when Ladd died in 1964.

Even in 1953 the road was one-way northbound, but there are no controlled pedestrian crossings as a bowler-hatted businessman crosses in the foreground, with a London 'bobby' strolling towards a road-sweeper's hand-cart further up. Today there are controlled crossings, and road markings are more explicit. There's an interesting comparison of taxi designs on the left. *C. F. B. Penley, A. Mott collection/WA*

The origin of the name **PICCADILLY** has never been established with certainty. It may be connected with a 'piccadill', a kind of stiff collar fashionable at the beginning of the 17th century; one supplier made his fortune from them and built himself a house in the area, nicknamed Piccadilly Hall. Alternatively, it may come from the Dutch word 'pikedillekens', meaning scraps or corners of a piece of cloth, this area then being the tip or corner of built-up London.

Whatever, by the middle of the 18th century this ancient thoroughfare (with Oxford Street one of the old routes westward from the City) was built upon as far as Hyde Park Corner. Since then the residential nature of the street has become a sought-after address for commercial offices and hotels, and virtually all the buildings are post-1860. On the right here at the eastern (Piccadilly Circus) end in October 1949 is the Piccadilly Hotel with its traditional coating of London soot (now cleaned as Le Meridien); built in 1905-8,

its frontage recedes behind a screen of giant columns (today the location of the glazed Terrace restaurant). The buildings beyond are in the course of demolition in 1949, and have since been replaced by modern offices, but still nicely in scale with the rest of the street. On the left in the 'present' view can be seen Simpson's famous store, built in 1935-6, the first welded steel building in London.

The broad unmarked roadway of 1949 features a queue of cars and taxis very much from the 'any colour you like as long as it's black' era, together with buses advertising 'Zesto Pickle', Swan Vestas and Borwick's baking-powder (the last two still very much with us in the 1990s). Adamson's Bedford lorry looks new. For some years Piccadilly has been one-way at the eastern end, although a 'contraflow' bus lane accommodates westbound buses. To avoid confusing unwary pedestrians, this is well marked and protected by substantial refuges with traffic lights. *London Transport Museum/WA*

As originally envisaged by Nash in 1819, PICCADILLY CIRCUS was indeed a Circus, formed by the crossroads of Regent Street and Piccadilly. However, in the 1880s the north-east corner, seen here in this view from the late 1950s (Disney's *Old Yeller* – advertised on the left – was released in 1957, and the Guinness clock, under scaffolding, was replaced in 1959), was destroyed to make way for Shaftesbury Avenue, and thereafter the Circus was more of an awkward triangle. Moreover, at the turn of the century the retailers on the northern side discovered the advantages of bright electric advertising hoardings, and the Bovril and Schweppes signs, erected in 1910, were a familiar feature of the corner of Shaftesbury Avenue for many years. On the opposite corner the new London Pavilion followed suit, soon becoming smothered in signs. On the south side of the Circus the Crown was landlord, and such advertising was not allowed.

The scene in 1996 shows many changes. Gone are Bovril and Schweppes, to be replaced by assorted Australian, American and Japanese products – not a British name among them! Gone too are the famous Guinness clocks (see overleaf). The Pavilion has

Trafalgar Square and Piccadilly Circus

been shorn of all its advertisements (for gin, disinfectant, chewing-gum, razors, petrol) and looks the better for it, newly restored and painted. The 1957 'do it yourself' road layout, with minimal markings and signs, was to change completely with the remodelling of the Circus in the 1980s.

A plan was unveiled in 1972 for the complete redevelopment of the Pavilion and Criterion sites, with towers linked by pedestrian decks. However, in the event the biggest change involved the famous statue of Eros being relocated to what is in effect a 'peninsula' rather than an 'island'! It was removed in 1985, returning in March 1986. Two years later, after restoration work, the statue and its fountain base, now moved some yards to the east, were unveiled once more. No longer having any pretensions of being a Circus, traffic now moves eastbound only round the top of the area. It certainly makes public access to the statue easier, as the steps around the base have always been a popular place to sit and watch the world go by. The new position is evident in the 1996 view, with traffic converging from Piccadilly (left) and Lower Regent Street (right). *N. L. Browne, courtesy of Frank Hornby/WA*

Whether or not the illuminated advertisements in **PICCADILLY CIRCUS** are considered an eyesore, they have certainly provided London with one of its most famous nightly attractions. These three views are of the corner of Piccadilly Circus/Glasshouse Street and Shaftesbury Avenue. The first, taken at 9.35pm on 24 June 1954, shows a Coca-Cola advert under erection between one for Ever Ready batteries and one of the famous Guinness clocks, complete with seals. These illuminated clocks were once a feature of many major cities, including Brighton, Bristol, Cardiff and Newcastle, and were derived from a famous poster of a clock face used to advertise Guinness. The first appeared in Piccadilly Circus in 1932; after a break during the war from 1939 to 1949, they were remodelled in 1954 and 1959.

Some time after the latter year, the second view shows a Double Diamond ad erected above the Coca-Cola one, and Forte's has opened a restaurant below. The new Guinness clock surmounts an ad for Morley nylons, while Bovril and Schweppes dominate the corner.

In 1996 the Saqui & Lawrence jewellers shop is now H. Samuel, the Guinness clock is gone and Coca-Cola has been squeezed up by McDonald's. The humble Ever Ready battery has been superseded by Japanese TV, video and fax; magnetic videotape was just beginning to be used in television recording in the 1950s, the first video recorder having been demonstrated in 1952, while fax was not widely available until the 1980s. A Burger King restaurant has replaced Forte's. *C. F. B. Penley, A. Mott collection/F. C. Le Manquais, courtesy of Tom Middlemass/WA*

This view of the eastern side of **PICCADILLY CIRCUS** on an unknown date in the 1950s shows clearly how effectively the London Pavilion has been restored – and how Eros has been shifted out of the picture altogether to its peninsula on the right! Built in 1885, the Pavilion was once a music hall and subsequently a theatre. Between 1934 and 1978 it was a cinema; later the inside was remodelled within the original facade, to be re-opened in 1988 by Margaret Thatcher. Its principal feature is now 'Rock Circus', 'Britain's No 1 Rock Attraction', complete with effigies of famous rock stars on the balconies. With such attractions as Alton Towers and Warwick Castle, it is part of The Tussauds Group, a far cry from when Marie Tussaud arrived in England from France in 1802 with 35 wax figures inherited from her uncle! It is described thus: 'Audio-animatronic moving and static wax figures, lasers, authentic memorabilia, videos, archive film and personal stereo sound surround you and astound you…' Like all great tourist venues, London has always used cutting-edge technology to attract visitors, and in its way Rock Circus is a direct descendent of Barker's remarkable 90-foot-diameter Panorama built 200 years earlier a few hundred yards away in Leicester Square.

As in the Circus itself, the advertisements on the corner of Haymarket in the right background have been reduced from Pan Yan pickle, Osram light-bulbs and BOAC to a single one for Hitachi.

The famous Eros statue, the first in London to be made from aluminium and dating from 1892, was intended to symbolise the Angel of Christian Charity rather than Eros the God of Love. It was erected by public subscription in memory of the reformer and philanthropist the 7th Earl of Shaftesbury. Since 1937 it has been boarded up to prevent invasion by New Year revellers, and during the war, from 1939 to 1948, it was kept in Egham, Surrey. *A. J. Pike, courtesy of Frank Hornby/WA*

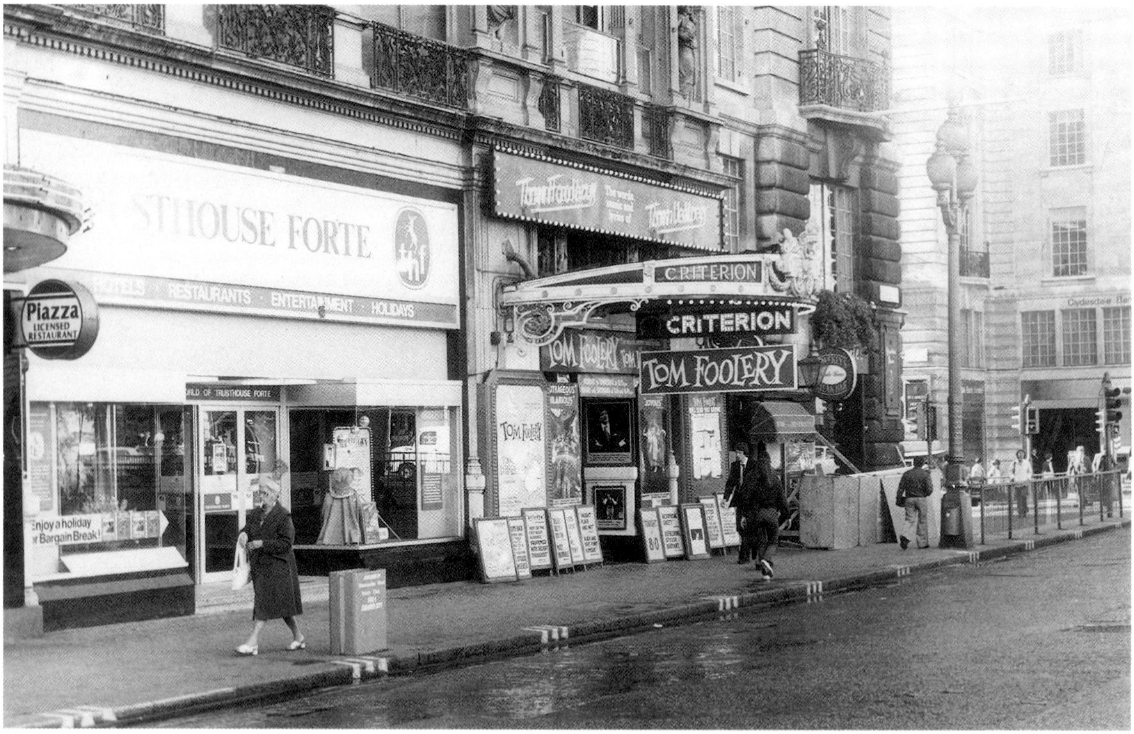
STHOUSE FORTE
HOTELS · RESTAURANTS · ENTERTAINMENT · HOLIDAYS
Piazza
LICENSED RESTAURANT
CRITERION
CRITERION
TOM FOOLERY
TOM FOOLERY
Enjoy a holiday
or Bargain Break!

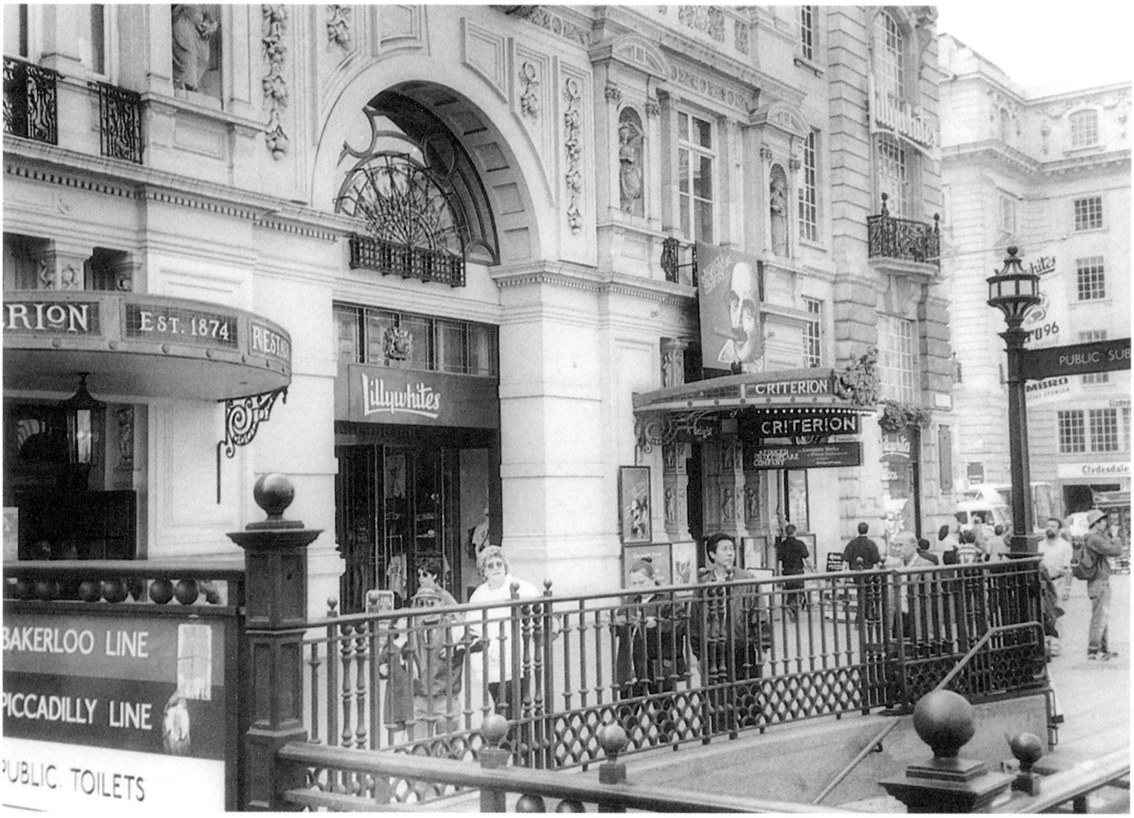
RION
EST. 1874
Lillywhites
CRITERION
CRITERION
PUBLIC SUB
BAKERLOO LINE
PICCADILLY LINE
PUBLIC. TOILETS

Left The Criterion Theatre stands on the south side of **PICCADILLY CIRCUS**, and the 'past' view, from about 1980, clearly shows the roadway on the south side of the island and relatively narrow pavement, now replaced by the broad 'peninsula' on which Eros stands, allowing space for an extra entrance to the underground station and pedestrian 'circus' (see overleaf).

The Criterion started life as the basement concert hall annex to the Criterion Restaurant, built in the 1870s, and was one of the first theatres to be constructed entirely underground. By the early 1980s the restaurant was empty, but recent redevelopment work has seen it re-open, with what appears to be a new entrance cut through to Lillywhite's famous sports store, where once was Trusthouse Forte's offices. Established by the son of 19th-century Sussex cricketer Frederick Lillywhite, the UK's largest sports shop has been on this site since 1925. The 'present' picture is neatly fixed in time by the banner announcing Euro 96.

The Criterion Theatre has a long tradition of comedy; in the 'past' photograph the show is *Tomfoolery*, featuring the words and music of American songwriter Tom Lehrer, whose satirical songs about drugs and atomic warfare made him one of the popular voices of the 1960s. The show was compiled by and starred Robin Ray, and featured perhaps Lehrer's best-known song, 'Poisoning pigeons in the park' (see page 29!). The 1996 hit is the 'Reduced Shakespeare Company' in *The Complete Works of William Shakespeare (abridged)* – the whole of the Bard in a single evening! *C. Mott, A. Mott collection/WA*

Right The Baker Street & Waterloo Railway (soon to be reduced to 'Bakerloo Line') was the first underground railway to cross central London from north to south, and opened in 1906. The same year the Piccadilly Line opened, and the two crossed at **PICCADILLY CIRCUS UNDERGROUND STATION**. In 1907 1.5 million people used the station, but by 1922 this had grown to a staggering 18 million (or some 49,000 people a day – a recent one-day survey gives today's figure as still over 44,000). The station was therefore rebuilt in 1924-8 with the entire booking hall underground. The Eros statue was temporarily removed to County Hall (and not replaced until the end of 1933) and the shaft to the works below sunk in its place. The new circulating area was not quite circular (having a diameter of between 144 and 155 feet), and the roadway above was supported on a 'spider's web' of steel girders and joists, amazingly with minimum disruption to traffic. Today the station still contains many of the design features of that rebuilding, as seen in the 'past' view dated 24 June 1959. The columns supporting the ceiling were of imitation stone with narrow brass fillets at the angles and twin lampshades at the top (removed in the 1959 shot, but since replaced). Set in the outer wall were stairways to the various street exits, basement shop windows for Swan & Edgar's department store (a famous Piccadilly Circus landmark until its closure in 1982), booking office, telephone booths and 26 automatic electric ticket machines. A couple of these are seen in the 1959 view, each issuing tickets to one fare value only. The pre-decimalisation fare and list of corresponding destinations is shown on the illuminated panel, with slots below for silver sixpence or one shilling coins, or 'coppers' (threepenny bits, pennies and halfpennies); presumably the machines were able to calculate and dispense change. The minimum 3d fare in 1959 was £1.10 in 1996, 88 times greater!

Modern-day electronics enable much more compact ticket machines; destination and type of ticket can be selected by the customer and an illuminated display shows the fare. Payment can be made by coin, banknote or even credit card; change is nearly always available. The tickets carry magnetic bands and are passed through automatic ticket barriers, which cancel them on exit to prevent a single-journey ticket being use more than once. Because flash photography is not permitted anywhere on the underground, the modern ticket machines seen here are those at Westminster station, at street level and open to daylight. *London Transport Museum/WA*

Lifts, escalators and stairs connected the booking area to the platforms. Shown here, possibly during the 1950s, is the northbound Bakerloo Line platform at **PICCADILLY CIRCUS UNDERGROUND STATION**. A Watford-bound train has just arrived, and passengers are alighting from a No Smoking carriage. Today, since the catastrophic fire at King's Cross underground station in 1987, smoking is banned on the whole of the underground system. At the end of the train can be seen the standard 'tube' tunnel ('tube' because they were bored though the ground and lined to a circular section, rather than the earlier sub-surface 'cut-and-cover' tunnels, which were of square section). The tube tunnels have a diameter of between 11ft 8in and 12ft 6in, while the station tunnels are just over 21 feet in diameter, accommodating on the Bakerloo a 291-foot-long platform. Originally, as seen here, the ceilings were plastered and whitewashed, broken with rings of tiles whose colours differed between stations so that regular users could more easily identify their destination.

Over recent decades the formerly rather gloomy aspect of the tube stations has been enhanced with lively decoration appropriate to each station, together with much improved lighting, both along the centre of the roof and concealed along the walls. A good example is Charing Cross station, also on the Bakerloo Line, seen here in the 'present' photograph. Details from works in the nearby National Gallery and National Portrait Gallery decorate the walls, while the new-style 'Next train' indicator not only shows the order of approaching trains, but also counts down the time in minutes before arrival, as well as being able to display other messages. So brightly lit are today's stations that this picture was able to be taken without the use of a flash. *London Transport Museum/WA*

ROYAL LONDON

PALL MALL formed the western exit from Trafalgar Square in Nash's 'great improvement' of the area from Carlton House to Regent's Park. It is seen here from the steps outside the National Gallery, the 'past' picture dating from Thursday 10 September 1953. On the left is Canada House, now cleaned and with a further storey added to its roof. Across the road the twin-towered building is Kinnaird House of 1915-22, and rising behind it the very inappropriate 225-foot, 15-storey tower of New Zealand House at the bottom of Haymarket, built in 1957-63.

In the right foreground the most dramatic addition to the scene, replacing what appears to be a post-war complex of single-storey shops, is the new Sainsbury Wing of the National Gallery. In 1985 brothers Sir John, Simon and Timothy Sainsbury offered to finance an extension to provide a home for the Gallery's collection of Early Renaissance works, as well as an auditorium, conference rooms, shop and restaurant. The various designs submitted provoked the Prince of Wales's famous 'carbuncle' remark, but that

accepted, by architects Venturi, Rauch & Scott of Philadelphia, USA, was completed in 1991. Standing in front is a statue of King James II. Note that the elegant gas-lamp standards of 1953 have been removed, but that a lamp has been replaced on the post beside the steps in the foreground. *C. F. B. Penley, A. Mott collection/WA*

PALL MALL We are now standing in the centre refuge of the pedestrian crossing in looking back towards Trafalgar Square, and at once the atmosphere of London's 'Clubland' is apparent – in the architecture and the cars! In June 1956, although virtually all the visible vehicles are Ford or BMC (Austin/Morris) products, it is the splendid Rolls-Royce on the left that catches the eye! In the 1996 view Fords and taxis still predominate, but we waited in vain to photograph a Rolls... The cyclist on the right – of which there are still many in London – is wearing a mask to filter the fumes.

In the distance can be seen the dome of the National Gallery, and Canada House to the right. In 1956, on the left, was the 'New Zealand Migration Offices', including the former premises of cigarette company 'Rothman's of Pall Mall' (with blind). Founded in

On the extreme right, the first building is the former United Service Club, built by Nash in 1827 immediately after the demolition of Carlton House and remodelled in 1842; in 1996, freshly repainted, it houses the Institute of Directors. Behind the camera Pall Mall proper starts at Waterloo Place, and beyond are the famous clubs such as the Athenaeum, Reform, Brooks's, Boodle's, etc. Note how the road markings in this one-way street have developed in 40 years. *London Transport Museum/WA*

Fleet Street in 1890 by Louis Rothman, whose family owned a tobacco factory in the Ukraine, the firm moved to Pall Mall in 1900 and is now further down at No 65. That whole block was replaced by New Zealand House. Next door to Rothman's is the arched entrance to Royal Opera Arcade (which still survives in 1996). This was London's first shopping arcade, and was designed in the Parisian fashion by John Nash and built in 1816-8.

Running parallel to Pall Mall is the famous processional route known as The Mall, leading from Trafalgar Square to Buckingham Palace. At its eastern end **ADMIRALTY ARCH** was erected in 1910 as the magnificent formal gateway from Trafalgar Square. The Latin inscription is King Edward VII's tribute to his mother, the Arch forming part of the national memorial to Queen Victoria. In this delightful 'past' photograph, taken in Coronation Year, 1953, the Arch is suitably decorated, and on the right, on both sides of the Arch, can be

seen some of the stands erected to accommodate 100,000 people, and containing 700 miles of tubular steel. The fashions of the day are well illustrated by the couple on the right, while heading towards the Arch on the left are, amongst others, a Citroen and an open-top Sunbeam. Today the cleaned Arch and refurbished buildings beyond produce a much brighter scene, although with no Coronation imminent in 1996! The central gates are only opened on ceremonial occasions. *N. L. Browne, courtesy of Frank Hornby/WA*

Pall Mall takes its name from a game of Italian origin, *palla a maglio* ('ball to mallet'), or *palle-maille* in French, which involved hitting a ball with a wooden mallet through a suspended iron hoop some distance away. 'A paille mall is a wooden hammer set to the end of a long staff to strike a boule with, at which game noblemen and gentlemen in France doe play much,' was a 1621 description. Pall-mall was once played by Charles II and his mistresses in the vicinity, then part of the park of St James's Palace, then in 1660 the alley was moved to a new half-mile-long, fenced-in, tree-lined site, and that eventually became **THE MALL**. Indeed, 'mall' eventually became a general term for any shady, tree-lined walk, and in our own time, via the USA, an undercover shopping precinct – the 'maul' of American TV!

In time The Mall became a popular promenading area for fashionable society folk, even after the game that gave it its name was no longer played. Surprisingly, however, the road that we know so well today only came into being in 1903-11. It was laid out as a 65-foot-wide route to the south of the original 'Mall' (now the parallel horse ride) joining Buckingham Palace with the new Admiralty Arch, at last solving the capital's embarrassing lack of a really impressive processional route.

Since 1911 many Royal occasions have including a procession along The Mall, and these are reflected in the accompanying pictures. In the first (*above left*) we see the 65-foot triumphal arches erected in May 1953 for the following month's Coronation. It was along here that the 2-mile-long procession, with its 10,000 marching men and women, came as the new Queen returned to Buckingham Palace on 2 June. Note the Irish-registered Ford Prefect in the bottom left-hand corner – perhaps over here for the celebrations?

On Friday 29 April 1960 (*left*) the banners are out to mark the Royal Wedding on 6 May of Princess Margaret and Anthony Armstrong-Jones (who became Lord Snowdon the following year).

In June 1977 the Queen's Silver Jubilee was another occasion for which The Mall was decorated (*top*). As for the Coronation, rain was a feature of the day, but as always it failed to dampen the spirit of the huge crowds. The Royal Wedding processions of Prince Charles and Lady Diana Spencer in July 1981, and Prince Andrew and Lady Sarah Ferguson in July

1986, also passed this way, but with the subsequent very public separations and divorces, the apparently changing attitude of the people to the monarchy, and its own perception of its future role in the light of recent self-reforming initiatives, will there be fewer such joyful occasions along The Mall in years to come?

The 1996 view (*above*) shows, of course, little change except perhaps in the growth of the trees, and road markings have appeared at the traffic lights at the junction with Marlborough Gate. *N. L. Browne, courtesy of Frank Hornby/C. F. B. Penley, A. Mott collection/WA (2)*

From the 16th to the 19th centuries **ST JAMES'S PALACE** was one of London's principal Royal residences (the only one when Whitehall Palace burned down in 1698). Originally built by Henry VIII in the 1530s on the site of a remote leper hospital, the only surviving part is the gatehouse (the clock and turret on the skyline) facing Pall Mall. The present-day buildings behind, seen here, are brick, built following a fire in 1809. Queen Victoria was the first monarch to move into the newly refurbished Buckingham Palace, but foreign ambassadors are still accredited to 'the Court of St James', although they are actually received at Buckingham Palace.

Perhaps not surprisingly, nothing has changed in four decades in this view looking up Marlborough Gate towards Pall Mall, except perhaps a few TV aerials; the lamp on the right is the same, and even the inspection cover in the pavement in front of it! The RT bus in the 1950s 'past' picture is on diversion, as no regular buses use Marlborough Gate. In 1996 it is replaced by two mounted police officers, while a party of American tourists, having 'de-bussed' in Pall Mall, make their way down to The Mall to see the Changing of the Guard. In the background can be seen the premises of Hardy's, makers of fishing tackle, established in 1872 in Alnwick, Northumberland, and located in Pall Mall since 1892. *A. J. Pike, courtesy of Frank Hornby/WA*

At the other end of **THE MALL** is the Queen Victorian Memorial in the centre of Rond Point, the 'circus' in front of Buckingham Palace. This was a product of the same Queen Victoria Memorial Committee that had instigated the Mall improvements. The area was to represent the 'hub of the Empire', and was designed by the same man who was responsible for Admiralty Arch and the new Portland stone frontage of the Palace. All was ready for the Coronation of King George V in 1911. The statue of Queen Victoria, facing down The Mall, is 13 feet high, made from a single block of marble and surrounded by allegorical figures such as Justice, Charity, Truth, Victory and Manufacture; the whole ensemble swallowed up well over 2,000 tons of stone. In the 'past' photograph, again dating from the Coronation of 1953, the statue is boarded round to protect it, and one of the triumphal arches can be seen as a mother and daughter venture gingerly into the road.

Car parking is certainly not encouraged in 1996, and the junction at Buckingham Palace is protected by traffic lights. Here, though, is at least one London thoroughfare where cars have no choice but to give way to horses, as a company of Guards process eastwards following the Changing of the Guard. Note how much cleaner the Palace is today. *Des Saunders/WA*

Despite being seen as the focal point of the British monarchy, **BUCKINGHAM PALACE** as a Royal residence is of relatively recent origin. Buckingham House was built in 1702-5 for the 1st Duke of Buckingham. In 1762 George III bought it for £28,000, but it was his son, George IV, who saw it as the new Royal residence, Carlton House being insufficiently grand; he engaged John Nash to repair and improve it. The work began in 1826, but when Queen Victoria came to the throne in 1837 it was still not really habitable. It was finally completed, with the construction of the 360-foot east front (to The Mall, giving Victoria and Albert more accommodation) in 1847; the enclosure of that front necessitated the removal of the former gateway – the Marble Arch – to its present site at the top of Park Lane (see page 79).

The Palace only received its familiar present-day frontage in 1913. Forty years later, in Coronation year, the Portland stone has suffered badly at the hands of the London atmosphere, but in 1996 it can once again present a clean face to the inevitable crowds who always seem to be there waiting for something to happen, or a glimpse of the Royal Family. In the 1993 view (*below left*) they will be unlucky, the absence of the Royal Standard on the flagpole indicating that the Queen is not in residence. The Guards protecting the Palace can be watched, of course, and most mornings the Changing of the Guard provides a fine tourist spectacle. Note in the 1953 and 1993 views the happy matching juxtaposition of the taxi and cars (in 1953 a Morris and an Austin Somerset, in 1993 a brace of Audis).

Even the 1993 view is now 'past', because in 1995 a 'pedestrian plaza' was created outside the gates; like Piccadilly Circus, Rond Point is no longer an island, with traffic travelling in both directions round one side only. 'How splendid,' said a spokeswoman for the Pedestrians' Association. 'Now that pedestrians are given priority and recognition in one of the seats of power, they will feel enthused to achieve the same in the towns where they live.' Some 17 million people go to the Palace each year, and in the previous three years 60 sightseers had been hurt in traffic accidents outside. The traffic lobby was less impressed, of course, but the development was awarded a Civic Trust commendation in March 1996.

Since 1993, to help pay for restoration following the disastrous fire at Windsor Castle, certain of the 600-odd rooms in the Palace have been open to the public for the first time. *Des Saunders/WA (2)*

Westminster

Left There's barely a brick or a chimney-pot to distinguish these two views, taken almost 40 years apart, of one of London's most venerable sites, **HORSE GUARDS PARADE**. The 1940 *Red Guide* describes it as 'the largest "clear" space in London (if a space can be described as "clear" which is largely used for the parking of cars)...' Our 1959 view shows no cars parked, and entry to the area for the few authorised vehicles in 1996 is strictly guarded. In 1959 it appears that stands are being erected, or perhaps dismantled, for the Trooping of the Colour, which has taken place annually here in June, on the monarch's official birthday, since 1805; the monarch also takes the salute. (The purpose of 'trooping the colour' is the parading of regimental colours in front of the troops so that they will recognise them on the field of battle.) The colours are those of the various Guards of the Household Division, and the Queen took the salute on horseback until 1986.

The area was used in Tudor times for tilting, and from the 17th century for parades of various kinds. The Horse Guards building itself was built in 1750-60, with what Pevsner refers to as its 'restless recessions and projections', surmounted by a clock tower; it is the headquarters of the Household Division of Guards and the London District Army Command. The buildings, from left to right, are Admiralty House (brick, 1780s), the former Paymaster General's Office, Horse Guards, Dover House, and the Cabinet Offices. Lord Wolseley and Lord Roberts survey the scene from their horses. *Frank Hornby/WA*

Right In its entry on **HORSE GUARDS**, the *Red Guide* continues: 'A passage under the picturesque clock tower ... is much frequented by foot-passengers, but only royalty and a few privileged persons on the Lord Chamberlain's list are allowed to drive through.' Certainly while we were attempting to take the 'present' picture we were interrupted by official cars entering through the gates from Whitehall, which were opened by the Life Guard who thoughtfully posed to take the place of the two 'squaddies' in the 12 September 1953 picture! In the lodges on either side of the gate, facing out into Whitehall, are mounted Horse Guards providing a famous and very patient tourist attraction!

Again the various buildings do not appear to have altered in the slightest degree in more than four decades. The building on the left with the circular columned corner is the old War Office of 1907, that on the right part of the Banqueting House begun by Inigo Jones in 1619; in the centre background is Whitehall Court, built as flats in 1884. *C. F. B. Penley, A. Mott collection/WA*

At the bottom of Whitehall is Parliament Street, leading into **PARLIAMENT SQUARE**, where this superb photograph was taken on Saturday 20 April 1957, looking north up Whitehall. Imposing government offices stand on the left, while on the right, on the corner of Bridge Street, is a building that has undergone an interesting transformation. It originally had a squat dome on the corner (*direction*, circa 1902) and gabled windows in the roof, but at some time prior to 1957 the upper storeys were removed and the very inappropriate tiled roof substituted. Then in 1991 the building was refurbished and upper storeys more in keeping with the original were replaced – the result is that the 1996 building looks more 'past' than the 'past' one! Where Noel's menswear shop was on the ground floor is now the Houses of Parliament book and souvenir shop. The buildings next door in Bridge Street have been demolished to

facilitate the construction of Portcullis House with the Jubilee Line Extension beneath it, and for the same underground work the Parliament Square island itself has been 'boxed in'.

The first 'traffic lights' in Britain were installed here in 1868; invented by a railway engineer, they stood 23 feet high, had semaphore arms attached and were controlled manually. In 1957 there's no sign of any, and a couple of policemen on point duty appear to be doing the job! In 1996 the traffic control is very complex, extending also to controlled pedestrian crossings. Security is also sophisticated, with a forest of surveillance cameras on the roof on the right, and a ban on unattended cycles. A traffic warden (introduced to London in 1958) also helps to keep everything moving! Note the BEA '1½-decker' airport bus in the 1957 photograph. *Frank Hornby/WA*

Is this the most famous view in London? Certainly the chimes of **BIG BEN**, via the radio, have symbolised home, civilisation, The Empire or whatever for many generations of Britons! Although popularly known by that name, 'Big Ben' is in fact the nickname only of the great hour bell, perhaps named after the Chief Commissioner of Works during the rebuilding, Sir Benjamin Hall. The clock mechanism is over 15 feet long and 4ft 7ins wide and weighs about 5 tons. The faces are 22ft 6ins in diameter and are made of translucent glass lit from white walls 5 feet behind them; the minute spaces are 1 foot square. The original cast iron hands were found to be too heavy for the mechanism to move, so were replaced by gunmetal ones. The minute hand still fell alarmingly when it passed the 12, so a lighter hollow copper one was used instead; it travels over 100 miles a year! The hour bell was cast at Whitechapel and weighs 13½ tons; the new hour begins on the last stroke.

The clock was started on 31 May 1859, and it used to take two men 32 hours to wind it every eight days until automatic winding was introduced in 1913. The 13-foot pendulum is regulated by adding or removing old pennies. Even the bombing of Parliament in 1941 only caused a 1½-second discrepancy! Three of the clock faces were reglazed in 1956, and in 1968 the 320-feet-high tower was found to be out of vertical by 9½ inches, but no further movement has been detected.

The 'past' view was taken at 4pm on Sunday 26 April 1959, so there's not a lot of traffic and, again, minimal traffic control. By contrast, at 4pm on Wednesday 29 May 1996 there's rather more! The 'Keep Left – one way only' sign reminds us that such arrangements are a relatively modern phenomenon, as described in the Introduction.

The pictures show again the new corner dome on the building on the left, and the old St Thomas's Hospital buildings across Westminster Bridge that have been replaced. *Frank Hornby/WA*

This is the east side of **PARLIAMENT SQUARE** looking south on Monday 12 July 1954. On the left is the vehicular entrance to the Houses of Parliament, and the roof of Westminster Hall, the only part of the original building to survive the disastrous fire on the night of 16 October 1834. The Hall was incorporated when the new Gothic Palace of Westminster was built; the foundation stone was laid in 1839 and the final part, the mighty Victoria Tower (seen here, 336 feet high), was completed in 1860. The part in scaffolding is the gatehouse-like St Stephen's Porch, the usual public entrance.

On the right is the east end of first St Margaret's church, today gleamingly cleaned, then the magnificent Henry VII's Chapel of Westminster Abbey, also now returned to its original glory (its elaborate architectural decoration inspired Pugin and Barry, the new Palace's designers). Note that since 1954 Millbank Tower of 1963 (see page 9) has appeared on the skyline. Traffic lights, road markings and the greater informality of the pedestrians' dress in 1996 are otherwise the main differences between the two views. *C. F. B. Penley, A. Mott collection/WA*

The north-east corner of the Houses of Parliament facing Westminster Bridge and the **VICTORIA EMBANKMENT** is the Speaker's residence, and it forms a distinguished backdrop to this photograph taken on 4 July 1952 during London's 'Last Tram Week'. All that week Londoners had been crowding on to the trams in an atmosphere of carnival mixed with sadness. Just before midnight on 5 July the last tram made its final journey from Woolwich to New Cross, cheered all along its route despite the hour. It arrived at New Cross half an hour late, and was driven into the Depot by the Deputy Chairman of London Transport, packed inside and completely surrounded by heaving crowds. However, while London's tram tracks now fell silent, 92 'Feltham' trams had been sold to Leeds at £735 apiece in 1950, and they continued in service until that city's tramway was in turn abandoned in 1959.

John R. Day, in *London's Trams and Trolleybuses*, sums up: 'The tram was in many ways even more the "people's transport" than the bus, partly because its cheap fares brought it into the reach of almost everyone. It was utilitarian for much of the time, its rails threw you off your bicycle, it occupied the centre of the street and refused to get out of the way, and yet we loved it. Its 6d fare to anywhere, after 18.00, could transform it into a magic carpet for the impecunious youngster wanting to explore his London. There was no thrill like that of a roaring, squealing, brightly lit tram rushing down a cobbled, gas-lit street on a slightly foggy winter evening. London is not the same without its trams and the older ones among us recall them with deep feelings…'

Note that the tram has a trolley pole on its roof, but that it is fastened out of use while current is being obtained via a collector running in a slot in the conduit in the road. When the tram reaches a point where overhead wires supply the current, the pole will be raised.

It is appropriate that the 'present' view of the same spot (where London's third horse tram route began in 1861) should show a further development in London's transport, the Jubilee Line Extension from Westminster to Docklands. The upper part of the Jubilee Line was built as the Fleet Line between Baker Street and Charing Cross via Bond Street, using part of the Bakerloo Line; it was renamed in 1977, and opened in 1979. In 1989 approval was given for the extension from Green Park to Stratford, east London. *London Transport Museum/WA*

In more relaxed times public car parking was permitted outside the Houses of Parliament in **OLD PALACE YARD**, but today security considerations mean that it is strictly controlled. On 22 September 1956 we can see a fairly new Mark 1 Ford Zephyr Zodiac and on the left a much older black Austin 10/4; today's cars are obscured by the metal railing.

Rising above them is the mounted statue of Richard I, the Lion Heart, and behind him Barry's magnificent window in the south wall of St Stephen's Porch, opposite the entrance to St Stephen's Hall and its great dais at the south end. The porch and lamps on the right mark the Peers' Entrance. Old Palace Yard takes its name from the original palace of Edward the Confessor, and it was here on 31 January 1606 that Guy Fawkes and his fellow Gunpowder Plot conspirators were executed. *Frank Hornby/WA*

This is the south side of **PARLIAMENT SQUARE**, looking towards Broad Sanctuary on the left, and beyond it Victoria Street; the date is 12 July 1954. Note first of all how the simple bollards at the junction with Old Palace Yard were all that protected cars and pedestrians; today the 'red and green men' and stout railings protect the unwary. Again, in 1996 the No Waiting sign and warning about leaving unattended pedal cycles remind us of modern security considerations.

In both pictures light vans are heading towards the Middlesex Guildhall of 1906-13. This was once the site of the Sanctuary Tower where fugitives from justice could find refuge, but this was abolished in 1623. Ancient Middlesex – the county of the Middle Saxons – lost much of its area to the County of London in 1888, and disappeared altogether in local government terms in March 1965, when it was absorbed into the administrative area of Greater London. However, quarter sessions are still held in the Guildhall. Glimpsed through the trees on the left is the

Methodist Central Hall (see page 64), and on the extreme left the tower of St Margaret's church. In 1996 the Parliament Square island is boarded off for the Jubilee Line Extension works. *C. F. B. Penley, A. Mott collection/WA*

In 1953 **WESTMINSTER ABBEY** is ready for the Coronation of Queen Elizabeth II on 2 June. The building against the West Front is the Coronation annex, designed by Ministry of Works architects; the entrance was at the left-hand side under the circular canopy beneath which hung a huge Royal coat of arms. It was here that the young Queen arrived in the magnificent State Coach to a roar of cheers and a fanfare of trumpets, despite the dreadfully wet weather, and from here that she departed to return to Buckingham Palace, wearing the Imperial State Crown and carrying the Orb and Sceptre; as her carriage left the Abbey the head of the procession, snaking through London, was already in Hyde Park, 2 miles away.

Back in May 1936 the Coronation of King George VI has been seen on television by a limited audience (from Cambridge in the north to Brighton in the south). The BBC Handbook of 1938 says: 'Mobile television was gloriously inaugurated on Coronation Day. Despite bad weather conditions, the whole of the Coronation Procession was televised from Apsley Gate, Hyde Park Corner, and it is estimated that more than 10,000 people found the opportunity to see the picture on a television screen…'

In 1953 many more were able to watch the event on TV, although there were only about 50,000 sets in Britain; 40 years later 98 per cent of British households possesses a television, of which 95 per cent are colour. Despite the technical limitations of the era, the biggest television audience to date sat enthralled by the chalky flickering pictures of the ceremony. There were establishment figures who were against the televising of the service, but those in favour prevailed.

The day ended with a night of celebrations, reaching their climax in a gigantic firework display on the South Bank, a highlight of which was a set piece portraying the Queen, the Duke of Edinburgh and their two children. For those without television, and who were used to seeing their news at the cinema, a full length Technicolor film was on release within days, narrated by Sir Laurence Olivier.

Although the Abbey dates from at least the 11th century – William the Conqueror was crowned here on Christmas Day 1066 – the great West Towers were not completed until 1745. The column in the foreground is a memorial to members of Westminster School who died in the 'Russian and Indian Wars'

of 1854-9, including Lord Raglan of Charge of the Light Brigade fame. Passing the column in 1953 is a splendid Triumph Roadster (familiar more recently from the TV series Bergerac), and parked next to it an L Series Vauxhall. After the Coronation, in 1954-6, a gift shop was established in front of the Abbey, but the most striking contrast between the two pictures is the cleaned stonework, which completely transforms the building – what a pity the atmosphere was not clean enough for it to be done in 1953! *N. L. Browne, courtesy of Frank Hornby/WA*

Looking across the open space beside Westminster Abbey, through which Broad Sanctuary passes diagonally, we can see the Methodist **CENTRAL HALL** in Storey's Gate. This was built in 1905-11 in the ornate French style, an early example of the use of reinforced concrete, giving it a distinctly continental look compared with the pomp and solidness of other institutional buildings in the area. It is noteworthy as the first meeting place for the infant United Nations in 1946.

Fifty years later the buildings flanking it have all been replaced; that on the left, formerly Abbey House of 1859 with its pavilion roofs, is now NIOC House, housing Barclay's Bank on the ground floor behind its elaborate detached concrete tracery, while on the right is The Queen Elizabeth II Conference Centre. Three of the five trees have survived the more than four decades since the 'past' picture was taken on 12 July 1954. *C. F. B. Penley, A. Mott collection/WA*

VICTORIA PANORAMA

WESTMINSTER CATHEDRAL in Victoria Street is the centre of the Roman Catholic Church in Britain, and while Victoria is only on the fringes of the area covered by this book, the view from the Cathedral's 273-foot-high campanile tower does afford spectacular views of many of the areas we have already visited, so the following panoramas are included for that reason.

The building was only completed as recently as 1903, designed in the Early Christian Byzantine style. Because finances were limited, the interior decoration was left for future generations to complete, a process still going on today. Development in Victoria Street led to demolition of property in front of the Cathedral in 1971, leaving an open area that allowed its distinctive frontage to be viewed fully for the first time. Because of its relatively recent date, the campanile contains a passenger lift, so taking the 'present' pictures was not so arduous a task for your authors as the laborious ascent of the spiral staircases of St Paul's and the Monument! WA

We start by looking north towards Buckingham Palace. In the 'past' view, dated (as all these are) Thursday 29 September 1960, the whole of the Palace can be seen (middle distance just to the left of the head of the crane); the older west front faces the garden, while at the right-hand end is the familiar east front, which completed the quadrangle in 1847. In front of the Palace can be seen the Queen Victoria Memorial surrounded by the gardens and ornamental gateways of Rond Point. The whole is backed by the trees of Green Park, bordered on the north side by Piccadilly.

The whole area on the north side of this end of Victoria Street was redeveloped between 1960 and 1966. The 6-acre site used to be occupied by Watney's Brewery, built about 1860 and demolished a century later in 1959. Bounding the site to the north-east is Palace Street with its Georgian cottages and assorted other buildings; the south side of the street was all demolished for the Stag Place development, which hides most of the view today. The building in the foreground is Esso House, which was eventually to swallow the remaining Victorian apartment block. Beyond the Esso flagpole on the extreme left can be seen the Hilton Hotel in Park Lane. On the right horizon is the British Telecom (formerly Post Office) Tower, opened in 1965. It has a total height of over 600 feet, and is 1¼ miles away from Westminster Cathedral (as we are told by the helpful plaques in each viewing gallery). *C. F. B. Penley, A. Mott collection/WA*

When Victoria Street was cut through the area of slums between Westminster Abbey and Victoria station between the 1850s and 1880s, it was remarkable for the evenness and uniformity of the height of its buildings. These were described as 'mansions', many divided into 'flats', a wholly new innovation in London at that time. Others contained blocks of 'chambers', many forming the offices of the prominent Victorian civil and mechanical engineering companies that built and supplied the railways. The five-to-seven-storey blocks are seen clearly flanking the street in the 1960 view, looking now north-eastwards; note the hundreds of chimney-pots that once contributed to the characteristic London 'pea-souper' fogs!

In the 1996 view the uniformity has been taken to extremes! Kingsgate House presents a blank face to Victoria Street, while tucked behind it in the bottom left-hand corner is the Gothic brick of Westminster City School. At the right of the picture is the 19-storey slab of Westminster City Hall. Bisecting the middle distance is the band of trees marking St James's Park. Just in front of them at the left-hand end is the long low rake of Wellington Barracks on Birdcage Walk, reconstructed in 1979-82. At the right-hand end in 1960 is the 14 storeys of 'that irredeemable horror' (Pevsner) known as Queen Anne Mansions, 'rudely bare … grimy brick walls and uniform windows'. It was built and part-designed by a property developer between 1873 and 1889, and mercifully demolished in 1971-2. The tallest building on the modern horizon is Centre Point. *C. F. B. Penley, A. Mott collection/WA*

In this and its companion volume we have already spoken of the horizontal layers of London, each age laying down new strata over the remains of the previous ones. These three views seem to demonstrate *vertical* layers, where successively taller buildings obscure the view of earlier ones behind. On 29 September 1960 (*above*) there is a clear view eastwards towards Westminster, characterised by the almost uniform scale of the major buildings. The large white block in the left middle distance is Broadway House, built in the late 1920s as the headquarters of London Transport. At 175 feet high, the clock tower made it at that time one of London's tallest and most 'modern' buildings! A little further to the right can be seen the large dome of Central Hall (see page 64), and above and slightly to the left the dome of St Paul's Cathedral, 1½ miles away. Right again the Shell Tower on the South Bank is under construction, then the tip of the tower of Big Ben can be seen directly behind the West Front of Westminster Abbey. The Houses of Parliament stretch as far as the Victoria Tower on the right. Directly beneath the Shell Tower, in Victoria Street, is the prominent 'crowning monstrosity' (Pevsner) of Windsor House (1880s), 'a nightmare of megalomaniac decoration', while the tiny building next door to it, on the corner of Buckingham Gate, is The Albert pub. In the centre foreground is the famous Army & Navy Store, linked by three footbridges to further premises in Howick Place.

By the date of the second photograph (*above right*, a close-up of the centre of a view taken on 23 July 1967), Victoria Street westwards has been entirely rebuilt, the Westminster City Hall block on the extreme left, then the ten storeys of Mobil House. In the centre middle distance is the 20-storey tower of the 'new' New Scotland Yard completed in 1966. On the skyline the Shell Tower was completed in 1963, and in front of Westminster Abbey in Victoria Street is the Department of Trade and Industry building, completed in 1964 and replacing Westminster Chambers of the 1860s.

The earlier views have by 1996 (*below right*) been almost entirely blotted out by a forest of new buildings. On the left Westminster City Hall is partly hidden and the rest of Victoria Street obscured behind the distinctive 'glass building-block' design of Ashdown House (undergoing refurbishment), while two new blocks now completely hide New Scotland Yard and the Shell Tower; both in Buckingham Gate, the dark one of the left is No 65, the Registered Office of Rolls-Royce Ltd, and the other is the modern-day Windsor House. Right again is Southside, the new 1977 building housing the Army & Navy, with just one footbridge across Howick Place.

Despite its present gleaming whiteness, Westminster Abbey is almost lost to view, while to the left of Victoria Tower can be seen the new block of St Thomas's Hospital across the river. On the far horizon is the City, a sierra of office blocks, of which St Paul's is the merest molehill! *C. F. B. Penley, A. Mott collection (2)/WA*

We are now looking roughly south-westwards towards the train sheds of Victoria railway station. In the foreground, running left to right, is Carlisle Place, then immediately behind it and parallel, Vauxhall Bridge Road. The light-coloured building in the left middle distance is the rear of the Apollo Victoria, formerly the New Victoria Cinema of 1929. Threatened with demolition in 1971, it was reprieved and now stages musicals and comedies. In 1996 Lloyd Webber's *Starlight Express* was the hit; the word 'Andrew' can be seen on the building in the 'present' picture.

Behind again are the roofs of Victoria station, which was in fact built as two stations side by side, one opened by the London, Brighton & South Coast Railway in 1860, the other by the London, Chatham & Dover Railway two years later. At the right-hand end of the station are the station offices, and behind them the French-style Grosvenor Hotel of 1861, one of London's first railway hotels, being cleaned in 1996. (Incidentally, Grosvenor is the family name of the Duke of Westminster, multi-millionaire landlord of the Belgravia area north of Victoria.) In the 1990s, as with other London railway termini,

Victoria Panorama

the value of the space above the platforms has been realised with the huge Victoria Plaza complex of shops, restaurants and offices. Whether Senior Service still satisfy cannot be told, since the building carrying the advert in Terminus Place and the trees in Grosvenor Gardens are obscured by more of the 'glass building-block' development (housing the headquarters of the John Lewis Partnership) along the south side of Victoria Street. The cluster of buildings on the right horizon of the 1960 view is the Victoria & Albert Museum, the dome of Brompton Oratory and the tower of Imperial College, over a mile and a half away. Finally, as a detail, note how the roof of the building in the centre foreground has been transformed by the addition of ducts and fans, presumably in connection with that modern luxury, office air-conditioning'. *C. F. B. Penley, A. Mott collection/WA*

Swinging the camera slightly to the right, and looking almost directly westwards, we are now back where we started. On the left, beside the Senior Service advert, is the very top of Victoria Street, at its junction with Buckingham Palace Road. The building on the right of the street with the domed tower is the Victoria Palace Theatre, built as a music-hall in 1911. It was the home of the Crazy Gang from 1947 to 1962, then the Black & White Minstrels, who gave almost 4,500 performances until 1970. While the gardens of Buckingham Palace, bordered by Grosvenor Place, can be seen in the top right-hand corner of the 1960 view, today the whole of the north side of Victoria Street and beyond has been redeveloped. Esso House is going up on the right, joined in the 1996 view (extreme right) by the 334-foot Portland Tower. The contrast between the flat roofs, chimney pots (what few remain in 1960!) and severe-looking brick rears of the earlier Victoria Street buildings and the delicate glazed blocks that have replaced them is fascinating, and epitomises London 'past' and London 'present'! *C. F. B. Penley, A. Mott collection/WA*

THE WEST END

The West End

Apsley House, the tall colonnaded building facing **HYDE PARK CORNER**, had the distinction in the early days of the post office of being known as 'No 1 London'. It certainly had a distinguished occupant, having been bought by the nation in 1820 for the Duke of Wellington in acknowledgement of his services. In the 1996 view his statue can be seen astride his faithful mount Copenhagen, who carried him at Waterloo, looking at his home from the island. Although 50 years ago the junction was not as forbidding an interchange as it is now, it could still be referred to in 1940 as 'one of the world's busiest traffic centres. Vehicular traffic passes the "Corner" on the gyratory system. A recent census shows that some 83,000 vehicles pass this point between 8am and 8pm – or nearly a hundred a minute.' A census in 1995 showed an average of 43,000 vehicles in 12 hours, a sizeable reduction.

Not much is passing on this day in March 1957, but that is explained by petrol rationing in the wake of the Suez Crisis, which erupted in July 1956. To the left of Apsley House is the 'screen' forming the ceremonial entrance to Hyde Park from Buckingham Palace via Constitution Hill, and to the right is the town house built for Lord Rothschild in 1862. At this date Park Lane was only a narrow road, entering Piccadilly off to the right of the picture. Then in 1961-2 Park Lane became a dual carriageway, was slewed to the west, the first few houses on the north of Piccadilly were demolished, and the new wide road entered Hyde Park Corner next to Apsley House, more or less where the No 16 bus is on the right of the 1957 photo (and to the right of the white lorry in 1996). The house, which today contains the Wellington Museum, was left rather marooned, and its newly exposed east side had to be re-faced. At the same time an underpass between Piccadilly and Knightsbridge was constructed to allow straight-through traffic to avoid the Corner, and the eastern entrance to this can be seen in the 1996 view; a labyrinth of subways connects the various roads and allows pedestrian access to the island. On the right is now the modern Hotel InterContinental, while in the distance can be seen the 1966 270-foot tower of Knightsbridge Barracks. *London Transport Museum/WA*

Following the road improvements, this is the eastern side of **HYDE PARK CORNER** on Wednesday 13 May 1964, with traffic from Piccadilly (right) merging with that circulating from the north side. The Routemaster bus is advertising Sheepdog Trials in Hyde Park over the Whitsun weekend, and coach-air fares to Paris apparently for £9! It can be seen that some of the older houses in Piccadilly survived, together with those on the east side of Hamilton Place, which was cut through in the 1860s to relieve the traffic bottleneck at the south end of the old Park Lane (off the picture to the right). The photograph is dominated by the newly completed Hilton Hotel in Park Lane, opened in 1963. It has 30 floors and over 500 bedrooms, with a rooftop restaurant and bar, one of the earliest in London.

By 1996 the buildings on the left have long gone, to be replaced by the Hotel InterContinental, which opened in September 1975, but some of those in Hamilton Place have survived, now overshadowed by the Londonderry House Hotel of 1964-9. One thing hasn't changed, and that is the continued use of the venerable Routemaster buses. The post-deregulation example here has reverted to the name 'London General', which was carried by many London buses from the mid-19th century until the formation of the London Passenger Transport Board in 1933. Road markings now aid the circulation round this complex interchange, while trees along Piccadilly and on the Hyde Park Corner island help to soften today's view. *London Transport Museum/WA*

A few years later, and the new **PARK LANE** is fully established. Originally it was literally just a lane outside the high brick wall that enclosed Hyde Park (off to the left in these views). In the 18th century a few houses began to appear along the east side, but it was not until the 1820s that it became a sought-after address. By the late 1930s Arthur Mee could write that the road was 'passing through a great transformation. A few of its old houses are still left but the old charm has passed away and vast hotels on the American scale have banished all remembrance of the days when this was one of the enjoyable walks in London.'

Yet greater change occurred at the beginning of the 1960s when it became a six-lane dual carriageway with a broad, leafy, but largely inaccessible central reservation, swallowing up a sizeable portion of Hyde Park. This 18 July 1969 view shows the southbound carriageway at the bottom end; originally Park Lane continued off to the right on the line of the old houses. The characteristic late 18th/early 19th century bow-window designs were originally the *rears* of the houses whose fronts are in Curzon Place, their back gardens once adjoining the park. Since being 'turned round', several of the bows have been modernised with almost full glazing. The modern building on the left on the corner of Curzon Street was built in 1963-5 for the Playboy Club (the first, complete with 'bunny-girls', was opened by Hugh Heffner in Chicago in 1960). On the extreme right can be seen the front of the Hilton Hotel. In 1996 we managed to catch a slightly quieter scene, and the No 16 bus approaching the extended bus lane is a modern rear-engined Metrobus. *London Transport Museum/WA*

MARBLE ARCH was designed by John Nash in 1828 as the gateway to Buckingham Palace (see pages 50-1), but it had to be moved when the new east front of the Palace was built; it was subsequently re-erected in 1851 at the top of Park Lane at its junction with Oxford Street, Edgware Road and Bayswater Road. It became the centre of a traffic island in 1908 and, if the 1940 *Red Guide* is to be believed, before the war saw 60,000 vehicles between 8am and 8pm; by 1995 only about 27,000 were recorded in a 12-hour census (of which only about 1,800 were heavy goods vehicles) – as with Hyde Park Corner, a substantial and welcome reduction.

In June 1952 a fine Coventry-registered Standard Vanguard 'Beetleback' and a trio of buses pass close to the south side of the Arch, in an area formerly separated from the road by railings. By 1997 it can be seen that the road has been pushed back further, leaving pleasant gardens around the Arch.

The position of the present road is shown in the third view; the 36 bus route is catered for by an RT in 1952 and an elderly Routemaster in 1997. This wider view allows a glimpse of the massive Cumberland Hotel above the Arch – this was built in 1933 and has nearly 900 bedrooms. *London Transport Museum/ WA (2)*

We now move into **OXFORD STREET**, which originally formed part of an old Roman way from Hampshire to Suffolk, and the more modern route between the heart of the City at Bank and Shepherds Bush in West London, thence to Oxford. Its name was established in the early 18th century when land to the north was coincidentally acquired by the Earl of Oxford – on a map of 1724 it was referred to as 'Oxford Street, the Road to Oxford'. Originally residential, by the end of the last century it was beginning to take on its modern guise with an influx of drapers and department stores. A post-war shopping guide for visitors describes the street as 'emphatically cosmopolitan in character; indeed, one may walk through it and emerge on the other side without having heard a single word of English spoken', which is of course still very much true today! So sought-after by retailers did it become that in the late 1930s space was rated at £30 a square foot.

There's not much of a gay, cosmopolitan air in this October 1949 photograph looking east from outside D. H. Evans's – it simply oozes post-war austerity! The wide, unattractive-looking street has a curious surface of what appears to be a brick-like paving, with metallic grips near the pavements – to aid horses' adhesion, perhaps? On the right a rag, waste paper and metal merchant's lorry is passing a parked railway delivery van that still carries its pre-nationalisation (1948) 'GWR' roundel and an advert for Torox beef cubes. On the first floor behind, 'Teen Togs' are being advertised – teenagers had probably only just been invented! The No 13 bus is advertising *Woman's Own* (first published in 1932), the one behind 'Wisk – does the big wash'.

In 1996 Oxford Street really does live up to its name as the capital's premier shopping street. Traffic – taxis and buses only – has been squeezed into the middle to allow for wider, more 'strollable' pavements, with stylish lamp standards carrying banners encouraging the wrapping and binning of chewing-gum (a major pavement-disfiguring problem today – those teenagers again!) and young trees. Most of the buildings on the south side survive.

In August 1996 bus shelters in Oxford Street were in the news when an advertising agency dreamed up the idea of marketing a new soft drink by installing infra-red sensors in ten bus shelter billboards; these detected the presence of a queue and released a spray of 'the flavour of a lemon orchard'. One wonders what the stern-faced overcoated 1949 shoppers would have made of such frivolity... *London Transport Museum/WA*

The Christmas shopping rush is well under way outside Selfridges in **OXFORD STREET** on Monday 8 December 1958 ('14 more shopping days' advises the notice on the window). The relatively narrow pavements are crammed with shoppers, many glancing at Selfridge's famous Christmas window decorations.

Gordon Selfridge opened his first store in Chicago in 1902, but sold up and came to Europe. Built in 1908-9, nothing like his colossal Oxford Street store, with its 500-foot frontage, had been seen in England before. The post-war shopping guide advises that, 'In this immense store there are over 200 different departments, and between them they cater for every imaginable need of civilised man…' ('from parasols to pineapples' as the 1940 *Red Guide* puts it). Arthur Mee describes how people smiled when Selfridge set up his great shop 'at the wrong end of Oxford Street where nobody came. People come today in their thousands and hundreds of thousands, and all the world knows Selfridge's…'

To compare December 1958 with May 1996 is perhaps not quite 'like for like', but Selfridge's is still one of the great Oxford Street stores. It now faces on to a wider, leafier pavement with benches for the weary shopper, the result of improvements completed in November 1993. The comparison of four decades of fashions is instructive! *London Transport Museum/WA*

THE WEST END

NEW BOND STREET was laid out in the 1720s by the Earl of Oxford as the northern continuation of (Old) Bond Street, named after Sir Thomas Bond, who owned the land in the 17th century. Ever an exclusive shopping street, after the war it was famous for jewellers, art galleries, auctioneers, tailors and couturiers. This is no less so today, although many of the names have changed with the fashions. The past view, looking from the corner of Brook Street up towards Oxford Street, was taken at 4.45pm on Saturday 6 October 1962, when Bond Street was open to two-way traffic; the Daimler, 4 DYR, perhaps contains a wealthy customer. Old Bond Street was even narrower than this, perhaps the narrowest of London's important streets and a notorious bottleneck.

Today it is one-way southbound, with three lanes of cars bearing down on the unwary shopper. Bennett's camera shop still sells photographic equipment under the Dixon's name, while Bentley the jeweller has become a shop for 'designer label' Guy Laroche. Hunt's (and upstairs the Lucie Clayton Model School) is now Escada, and beyond there are two furriers, at a time when such things were less frowned upon; the lady on the corner in the foreground sports an expensive-looking fur jacket, and clutches handbag, gloves and a neatly covered umbrella (perhaps she won 'more on Copes', as the bus advises us!). Further up there is one of Carwardine's restaurants for tea and coffee.

The 'past' photograph was taken from the first floor of what is now an Armani shop – your photographer, in baggy-kneed jeans and charity shop jacket, felt that a pavement-level shot would do the job perfectly adequately... *London Transport Museum/WA*

OXFORD CIRCUS forms the intersection of Oxford Street and Regent Street. The four quadrants are of identical design and date from between 1913 and 1928 – one was heavily bombed during the war but was repaired. This 'past' view was taken from the first floor of Peter Robinson's store looking west along Oxford Street between 9.30am and 10.00am on Thursday 23 September 1954. As the post-war shopping guide tells us, 'furs strike the dominant note and fill the windows – on the northern side is Swears & Wells, and in the other corner, Jays, renowned also as a dressmaker.' (The fourth corner was occupied by Spirella corsets.) Yorkshireman Peter Robinson opened his first shop on this site in 1833; part of the Burton Group since 1946, today it carries the name Top Shop. Real furs have now, of course, gone; on the left is now Benetton, on the right Hennes & Mauritz.

Familiar names like Saxone and Salisbury's can be seen in the 1954 photograph, as well as period detail such as a shop selling 'gowns and mantles'; there's also a branch of the 'Fifty Shilling Tailor'. The buses are advertising the *News of the World* ('War-time secrets that can now be told'), Weston's biscuits, and *This is Cinerama*, the first Cinerama film, released in 1952 and showing at the London Casino (now the Prince Edward Theatre). The cobbled paving of the Circus can be seen, together with minimum traffic control and no pedestrian protection.

The 1996 view (which could not be taken from upstairs) shows that while the buildings still maintain the 'Circus' shape, the originally concave segments of the pavement have become convex, protected by stout balustrades, making the road more of a conventional crossroads in shape and allowing space for entrances to the subways and underground station. The walls also provide an ideal place to sit, to see and be seen! No motor vehicles except buses and taxis are allowed in Oxford Street today, and the pedestrian crossing has lights and protective barriers on the central refuge. *London Transport Museum/WA*

Here is another aerial view that unfortunately could not be exactly replicated, looking from Oxford Circus southwards down **REGENT STREET**. Dated April 1955, it shows such a wealth of period vehicles that it seemed a pity not to include it! Amongst them is a lorry carrying sacks of coal (not much demand for that in central London today!), a Scammell 'mechanical horse' three-wheeled British Railways delivery dray, and a wide variety of cars and vans, every one of which would today make a vintage vehicle collector's mouth water! The shops include Spirella corsets on the extreme left, then Helen Kaye ladies' fashions, London Shoe, Dr Scholl's and a branch of the National Provincial Bank (in 1968 becoming a constituent of the NatWest). Then follows Dickins & Jones store, established in Oxford Street in 1790 and still a feature of Regent Street today.

Regent Street was part of John Nash's grand design for a *Via Triumphalis* (Triumphal Way, or 'New Street', as it was originally referred to) from Carlton House to Regent's Park. It was cut through amidst much upheaval in the early 18th century, but by the 1920s had been almost entirely rebuilt, leaving us the street as we know it today. It is impossible to read the newspaper hoarding held by the white-coated vendor outside Jay's in 1955, but in 1996 the *Evening Standard* is leading with a story about footballer 'Gazza' (Paul Gascoigne). The new entrance to Oxford Circus underground station reminds us that this is not just an important junction above ground; beneath the Circus is the interchange between the Central Line (running beneath Oxford Street and opened in 1900), the Bakerloo Line (running north-south beneath Regent Street and opened in 1906) and the Victoria Line (which opened in 1969 and to accommodate which the station was rebuilt). *London Transport Museum/WA*

The West End

One of London's most famous variety theatres, the **PALLADIUM** is tucked away behind Oxford Circus in Argyll Street. It opened in 1910 as a luxurious music-hall, and became officially known as the London Palladium in 1934. It is perhaps best remembered as the venue for the live one-hour TV show *Sunday Night at the London Palladium*, which was a weekly event from 1954 to 1965, and was revived less successfully in the early 1970s. Comperes included Tommy Trinder, Bruce Forsyth, Norman Vaughan and Jim Dale. TV critic Philip Purser described it in 1959 as 'one of life's reassuring certainties. Cheery compère will succeed high-stepping girls; "Beat the Clock" will follow a couple of lesser turns; finally there will be the Big Star, and all the lush splendour of the revolving-stage finale.'

From Saturday 4 October 1980, according to the 'past' photograph, the theatre is presenting American entertainer Lynda Carter, who had enjoyed success on television in the late 1970s as 'Wonder Woman'. Forthcoming attractions include 'Britain's foremost entertainer', Max Bygraves, and the Four Tops, the 1960s Motown chartbusters who in 1981 were to experience a revival of fortunes with their first UK Top 3 hit in ten years.

Jim Dale returned to the Palladium in 1994, receiving critical acclaim as Fagin in a revival of Lionel Bart's famous musical *Oliver!*, first performed in London at the Albery Theatre, St Martin's Lane, from 1960 to 1966 in a record run of 2,618 performances; it was revived again in 1977.

The Palladium is currently owned by Stoll Moss Holdings; as can be seen from the van delivering potted plants, that company is also the proprietor of the Queen's, Gielgud, Apollo, Lyric, Her Majesty's, Garrick, Cambridge, Theatre Royal, Royalty and Duchess theatres. It was announced in September 1996 that multi-millionaire musical producer Cameron Mackintosh, who is responsible for *Oliver!*, might be about to bid for seven other West End theatres currently owned by Mayfair Theatres & Cinemas – the Piccadilly, Comedy, Wyndham's, Albery, Phoenix, Whitehall and Donmar Warehouse (he already owns the Prince of Wales and Prince Edward). It was felt that the West End would benefit from so many theatres being owned by someone who actually puts on productions. *C. Mott, A. Mott collection/WA*

Parallel with Lower Regent Street, heading down from the east side of Piccadilly Circus, is **HAYMARKET**; in the 17th century the Royal Mews were nearby towards present-day Trafalgar Square, so hay and straw would have been in demand. This road is one-way southbound, as the sign on the lamp standard to the right of the October 1953 'past' photograph tells us. Halfway down is what was originally the Carlton Theatre of 1926; converted to a cinema in 1929, it was sold to Paramount in 1930, and is now owned by MGM, with three screens. Parked outside in 1953 is a sleek Armstrong Siddeley.

The 1953 presentation is *The Man Between*, described by film historian Leslie Halliwell as an 'imitation *Third Man* [which Reed had also directed, in 1949] with an uninteresting mystery and a solemn ending. Good acting and production can't save it.' The same year James Mason had played Brutus in *Julius Caesar* with John Gielgud and Marlon Brando, while *The Man Between* was only the fourth film of 22-year-old Claire Bloom. The more graphic advertising of the film is in contrast to the 1990s style of illuminated panel with titles only. Also by contrast is the nature and tone of today's films: *Trainspotting* (18), a tale of Edinburgh drug addicts described by the film magazine *Empire* as 'the best British film of the decade ... dark and dirty, violent and mean, but ... also violently affecting...'; *Things To Do In Denver When You're Dead* (18) (starring Andy Garcia, not born until 1956), a quirky crime film; and *Kids* (also 18), 'a loose semi-documentary about New York's teen youth'. Despite being the story of a West Berlin racketeer and double agent whose death arises from his love for Claire Bloom, *The Man Between* still rates a U certificate – one can imagine that the treatment today would certainly bring it into the 15 or 18 category... C. F. B. Penley, A. Mott collection/WA

The **WINDMILL THEATRE** was a London theatrical institution. Named after its location in Great Windmill Street (off Shaftesbury Avenue), itself named after a windmill that stood here until the late 18th century, it was built in 1910 as a cinema, the Palais de Luxe. It became a theatre in 1931, and the following year general manager Vivian Van Damm introduced his 'Revudeville', a non-stop variety show that ran from 2.30pm to 11pm every day, and was famous for its nearly-nude tableaux (the girls were required by law to remain motionless). 'Any additional artificial aid to vision is NOT permitted,' warns a 1949 programme. 'All scenes presented at this Theatre are fully protected and must not be photographed or reproduced…' As it was a continuous performance, the management reserved the right to re-sell any seat left vacant for more than 15 minutes. Apart from a couple of weeks in 1939, the Windmill was the only theatre in London to stay open during the Second World War, hence its proud 'We Never Closed' slogan.

Van Damm died in 1960, and his daughter ran the theatre until 1964, when it finally did close and reverted to a cinema. In 1973 it was acquired by Paul Raymond, who returned it to its former – and by this time more explicit – role. In this guise it is seen here in about 1980, presenting *Rip Off!*, 'Live on stage … full frontal sexual exposure … the erotic experience of the era'. But by 1981 it was closed again, and since then has had a chequered history as a theatre restaurant until 1986, thereafter the Paramount City Theatre, again for nude shows and variety, and currently as a discotheque under the same name.

A row of the familiar red telephone boxes can be seen on the right in both pictures. Their survival in the 1990s is the subject of heated debate. English Heritage warned of 'visual chaos' as less than ideal new BT designs and those of rival companies proliferate; in 1996 it organised a meeting between the phone companies and the Royal Fine Art Commission to suggest a competition to come up with a worthy successor to architect George Gilbert Scott's classic 'K6' design. Meanwhile, Westminster City Council has decreed that the familiar red box must be retained in historic locations. *C. Mott, A. Mott collection/WA*

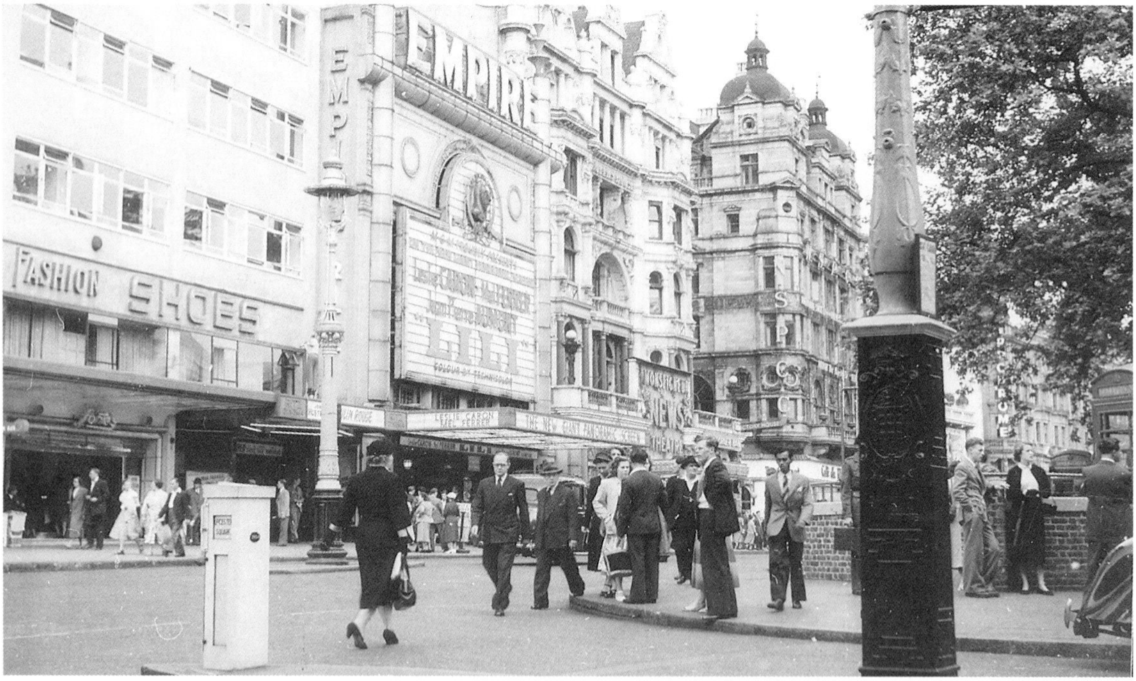

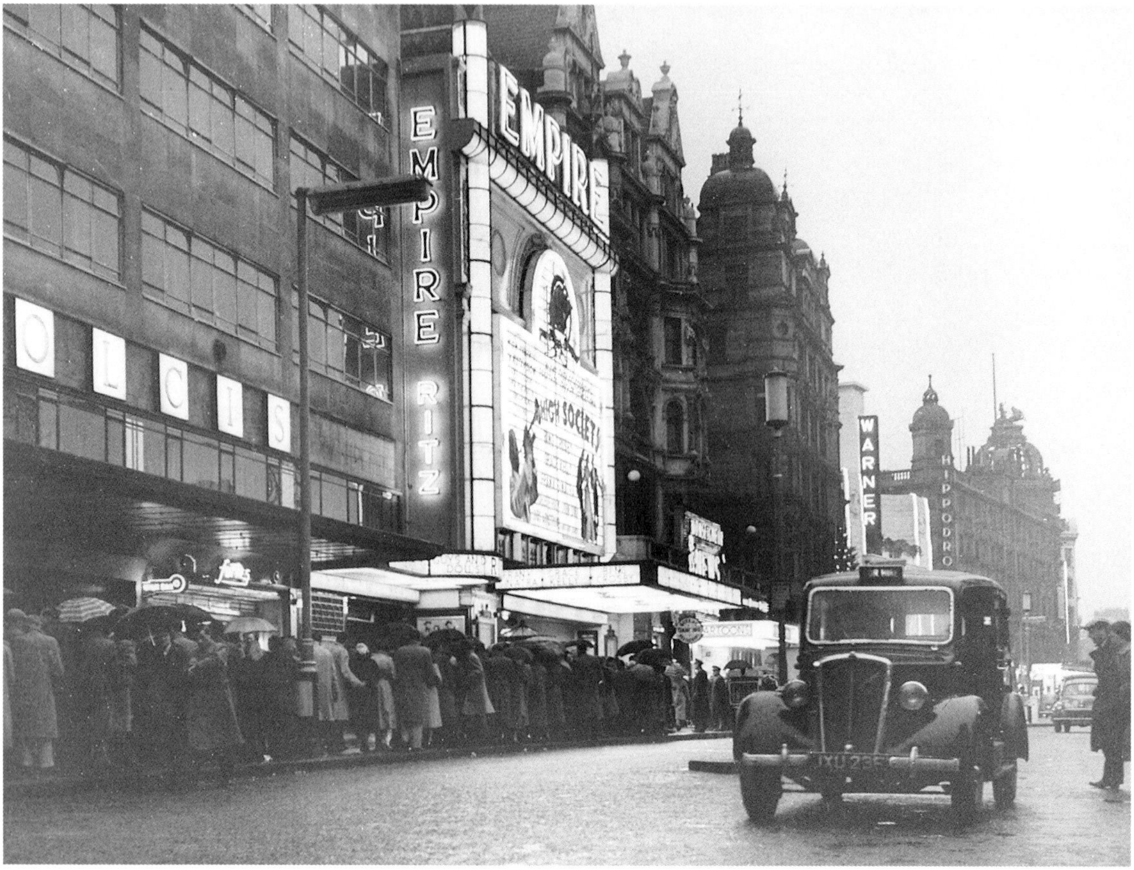

The land around **LEICESTER SQUARE** was acquired in the 17th century by the 2nd Earl of Leicester, who built Leicester House on what is now the north side of the Square; one of the largest houses in London, it was demolished in the 1790s. During the 19th century the Square began to take on the character familiar today, as a general centre of entertainment. Occupying the north side of the Square since 1928 is the Empire Cinema, built on the site of the Royal London Panorama; in 1884 this had been rebuilt as the Empire Theatre, which became a music-hall in 1887 and was pulled down in 1927. The 1953 view (*above left*) shows the Square when traffic circulated around it, and the Empire's feature presentation is *Lili*, a 'romantic whimsy' starring Leslie Caron and Mel Ferrer. Note the MGM lion above the main hoarding.

The second view was taken on the wet evening of Sunday 16 December 1956, and is an atmospheric and nostalgic reminder of when queuing for the 'one and nines' along the pavement under umbrellas was a national pastime! The film is *High Society*, with Grace Kelly, Bing Crosby and Frank Sinatra (a musical reworking by Cole Porter of the much better *Philadelphia Story* of 1940, starring Katharine Hepburn and Cary Grant). On the left is the Dolcis building of 1937, in the 'anonymous modern idiom, just with band upon band streamlined round a rounded corner' (Pevsner). In the right background can be seen the Warner cinema of 1938 ('wildly modernistic') and beyond that the Hippodrome, later the Talk of the Town.

The 1996 view (*above*) shows the now pedestrianised Square. The Empire's modern canopy is rather garish, but the removal of the hoarding has revealed the dramatic 1920s picture-house architecture behind. *C. F. B. Penley, A. Mott collection (2)/WA*

Warner Leicester Square presentations, 1950: *Colt .45* starring Western stalwart Randolph Scott (who died aged 89 in 1987), and *Night Unto Night*, a 'cheerless nuthouse melodrama' (Halliwell) with 39-year-old Ronald Reagan, who 30 years later would become President of the United States…

Many of the photographs in this book were taken by Charles Penley, who during the 1950s and 1960s was manager of the Empire Cinema in **LEICESTER SQUARE**. Born in 1894, he was the son of W. S. Penley, who played the original title role in *Charley's Aunt* (and may have been Brandon Thomas's co-author). Before taking over at the Empire, Charles Penley was a theatrical producer, putting on many shows. Some of his many photographs of the Empire are shown here.

To compare a snowy Tuesday 2 March 1954 with a sunny May day in 1996 is not really fair, but it is clear that the gardens have changed quite a bit. They were originally Lammas land, available free to parishioners for drying clothes and pasturing cattle after Lammas Day (12 August). For many years until the last century they were criticised for their dilapidated state, until bought for the public in 1874 and laid out with the fountain and statue of Shakespeare in the centre, and busts of other great men who had once lived in the Square. Over a century later a delightful statue of Charlie Chaplin was added (unveiled by Sir Ralph Richardson in 1981). Even since the war Leicester Square has been described as 'the dullest of all our famous squares', and was in recent times a haunt of vagrants and 'winos', but at long last has been refurbished, being re-opened by the Queen in June 1992.

In this 1954 view the Empire's main feature is *Kiss Me Kate*, starring Howard Keel and Kathryn Grayson; this was the 3-D screen version of the Broadway hit based on Shakespeare's *The Taming of the Shrew*. There's 'real' Shakespeare next door at the Ritz in the form of *Julius Caesar* (already referred to on page 88). On the right is the Monseigneur News Theatre; these were once popular in London as a continuous programme of news and cartoons in the days before almost universal television ownership. *C. F. B. Penley, A. Mott collection/WA*

The more sharp-eyed among you will have noticed on the previous pages that immediately next door to the Empire in Leicester Square was the **RITZ CINEMA**, the entrance to which was on the ground floor of the Dolcis building. On Thursday 13 May 1954 it is, like the Empire, boasting a 'new panoramic screen' (this was the era of 'wide screen entertainment', Cinemascope having been copyrighted by Fox in 1953 and imitated by others). *Knave of Hearts* concerned a philanderer (played by France's leading young romantic actor of the 1950s, Gerard Philipe, who was to die of a heart attack in 1959 before his 37th birthday) confessing his affairs to his wife. As a sex comedy is was somewhat pioneering for its day, and the poster clearly states that its X certificate means 'definitely adults only'.

In 1996 the Ritz was no more, the premises being occupied by a branch of Baskin Robbins, the American ice-cream company; the first floor of the Dolcis building was a restaurant, while the former Forte's restaurant was a branch of the Deep Pan Pizza Co, once again demonstrating the cosmopolitanism of modern London! *C. F. B. Penley, A. Mott collection/WA*

Above On the opposite (south) side of Leicester Square is the former **LEICESTER SQUARE THEATRE** of 1930, now the Odeon West End. Back in 1953 the cinema was advertising the European première of Disney's *Peter Pan*. Critics objected to Disney's interference with the plot (as he had also done with *Alice in Wonderland* two years earlier), and his use of the voice of 16-year-old American boy star Bobby Driscoll as Peter (he was another film actor who was to die young, in 1968 aged 31, in poverty and a drug addict). As a recent critic said, 'If you can view it without thinking of Disney messing [not the actual word used!] about with yet another children's classic and relax in the studio's last decent use of Technicolor, then you're in for a treat.' The supporting short, *Nature's Half Acre*, was one of Disney's celebrated live-action 'True-Life Adventure' series, which won the Oscar as best two-reel short at the 1951 ceremony, hence the statuettes on the hoarding. Parked outside the cinema is a Hillman Minx convertible, and in the foreground a 'razor-edge' Triumph Renown.

Not only the Toys but also Walt Disney Pictures are back in town 43 years later! State-of-the-art animation in 1996 is represented by Disney's *Toy Story*. Having made the first full-length animated feature, *Snow White and the Seven Dwarfs*, in 1937, this was the first ever full-length computer-animated feature. As the *Empire* magazine reviewer commented, 'The result proves so breathtaking that two-dimensional cartoon fare will never seem the same again and offers further, glorious proof that movies aimed at junior cinemagoers are quite often miles better than those directed at their parents.'

Back in 1953 Leslie Nielson was about to make his first film. He made his name playing rugged cops or similar, until in *Airplane* (1980) and later *The Naked Gun* (1988) he revealed a great talent for straight-faced playing in zany comedies, although critics felt that *Spy Hard* was perhaps a spoof too far... *C. Mott, A. Mott collection/WA*

Right The **ODEON CINEMA, LEICESTER SQUARE** celebrated its 60th anniversary in 1997, its 'black and showily austere' frontage (Pevsner) having been built in 1937 on the site of the Alhambra theatre. From its opening in 1854 until its demolition in 1936, the Alhambra saw a varied succession of entertainment from circus and music hall to revue, ballet and opera. This very snowy view, taken by Mr Penley from the upper storeys of his Empire cinema in 1954, shows the film on release to be Norman Wisdom in *One Good Turn*. Londoner Wisdom left school at 14 and made his first stage appearance at Collins's Music Hall in Islington in 1946. This was his second film, but unlike the first, *Trouble in Store*, it was an 'unmitigated disaster' (Halliwell). However, that didn't stop Norman Wisdom going on to enjoy a long and successful career, being Britain's biggest comedy star until the mid-1960s. Note that his co-star is another stalwart entertainment veteran, Thora (now Dame Thora) Hird. Some parked cars, a motor coach, a taxi and a cabmen's bothy complete this very atmospheric scene.

For many years the Odeon has played host to important cinema events, including the Royal Film Performance. In the late 1990s it was refurbished, its familiar black 1930s exterior retained but a glass-panelled frontage and balcony cut into its entrance. In 2000 the main film on offer is Tom Hanks in *The Green Mile*. The staid 'Quality Inn' and 'Good Food' advertised next door in 1954 has given way to a huge banner advertising the refurbishment of the Chiquito restaurant. Pedestrianisation has transformed this side of the Square, and the cabmen's shelter is a long-disappeared relic of the past. *C. F. B. Penley, A. Mott collection/WA*

INDEX

Admiralty Arch 44-7
Albert Embankment 9
Apollo Victoria theatre 72-4
Apsley House (Wellington Museum) 76
Argyll Street 87
Army & Navy store 70-1
Ashdown House 70-1

Big Ben (see also Houses of Parliament) 56-7, 70-1
Bridge Street 54-5
British Telecom Tower 66-7
Broad Sanctuary 61, 64
Broadway House 70-1
Brook Street 83
Buckingham Palace 28, 46-7, 50-1, 66-7, 72-3, 79
Buses 77, 79

Canada House 26-8, 41, 42-3
Carlton cinema 88
Carlton House Terrace 20-21, 41
Cecil Hotel 24
Centre Point 22-3, 68-9
Charing Cross Pier 22-3, 24
Charing Cross Road 26-7
Charing Cross station 25
Coliseum theatre 29
County Hall 12-13, 14, 22-3
Criterion Theatre 38
Curzon Place 78

Department of the Environment building 18-9
Dickins & Jones store 86
Downing Street 20-1
Duncannon Street 26-7

Embankment Pier 24
Embankment Place, No 1 22-3, 25
Empire cinema 90-92
Eros statue 34-9
Esso House 66-7, 74-5

Festival of Britain 22-3

Great Windmill Street 89
Grosvenor Hotel 72-3

Guinness clocks 34-6

Hamilton Place 77
Haymarket 37, 41, 88
Hilton Hotel 20-1, 66-7, 77, 78
Horse Guards Parade 52-3
Hotel InterContinental 76-7
Houses of Parliament (see also Big Ben) 11, 12-2, 16-7, 18-9, 30, 58-60, 70-1
Hungerford Bridge 22-3, 24
Hyde Park Corner 76-7

Kingsgate House 68-9

Lambeth Bridge 9, 10, 11, 16-7
Lambeth Palace/Pier 10, 11
Leicester Square 90-95
Leicester Square Theatre (Odeon West End) 94
Lillywhite's 38
Londonderry House Hotel 77
London Hippodrome 90-1
London Pavilion 34-5, 37
Lower Regent Street 31, 34-5

Mall, The 20-1, 44-7, 49
Marble Arch 50-1, 79
Marlborough Gate 46-7, 48
Methodist Central Hall 18-9, 61, 64, 70-1
Middlesex Guildhall 61
Millbank/Tower 9, 11, 16-7, 58
Ministry of Defence building 20-1
Mobil House 70-1

Nash, John 31, 34-5, 41, 42-3, 50-1, 79, 86
National Gallery 26-7, 28, 41, 42-3
Nelson's Column 30
New Bond Street 83
New Scotland Yard 12-3, 18-9, 70-1
New Zealand House 26-7, 41
Northumberland Avenue 30

Odeon, Leicester Square 95
Old Palace Yard 60
Oxford Circus 83-7

Oxford Street 79-82, 84-5

Palace of Westminster, see Houses of Parliament
Pall Mall 26-8, 41-3, 46-7, 48
Palladium Theatre 87
Park Lane 76-8
Parliament Square 54-5, 58, 61
Parliament Street 54-5
Peter Robinson's stores 84-5
Piccadilly 30-3, 66-7, 76, 77
Piccadilly Circus 34-40; underground station 39-40
Piccadilly Hotel (Le Meridien) 32-3
Players Theatre 25
Plaza cinema 31
Portcullis House 12-3, 18-9, 54-5
Portland Tower 74-5
Poultry, No 1 6
Post Office Tower, see British Telecom (BT) Tower

Queen Anne Mansions 68-9
Queen Elizabeth II, coronation 46-7, 62-3; Silver Jubilee 46-7
Queen Elizabeth II Conference Centre 64
Queen Victoria Memorial 49, 66-7
Queen Victoria Street 6

Regent Street (see also Lower Regent Street) 34-5, 83-6
Ritz cinema 93
Rond Point 49, 50-1, 66-7
Royal Opera Arcade 42-3

St James's Palace 46-7, 48
St James's Park 20-1, 68-9
St Margaret's, Westminster 18-9, 58, 61
St Martin-in-the-Fields 26-8
St Martin's Lane 26-7
St Mary-at-Lambeth 10
St Paul's Cathedral 70-1
St Stephen's Hall, Westminster 60
St Thomas's Hospital 14, 16-7, 56-7, 70-1

Savoy Hotel 12-3
Selfridges 82
Shaftesbury Avenue 34-7
Shell Centre 9, 15, 70-1
Shell-Mex House 24
South Africa House 29
South Bank 15
Strand 22-3, 24, 30
Swan & Edgar 39

Talk of the Town, see London Hippodrome
Tate Gallery 9
Telephone boxes 89
Temple of Mithras 6
Thames, River 9ff, 15ff
Thames House 9
Trafalgar Square 18-9, 26-30
Traffic management and flows 26-7, 54-5
Trams 59

Underground railways, Bakerloo 39, 59, 86; Central 86; Jubilee 18-9, 54-5, 59, 61; Victoria 86
United Service Club 42-3

Victoria Embankment 9, 12-3, 18-23, 59
Victoria Palace Theatre 74-5
Victoria station/Plaza 72-3
Victoria Street 18-9, 61, 66-75
Villiers Street 25

Wellington Barracks 68-9
Westminster (RC) Cathedral 18-9, 66-75
Westminster Abbey 12-3, 18-9, 58, 62-4, 68-9, 70-1
Westminster Bridge 11, 12-3, 16-7, 18-9, 22-3, 56-7, 59
Westminster City Hall 68-71
Westminster City School 68-9
Westminster Hall 12-3, 58
Westminster Pier 12-3, 18-9
Whitehall 18-9, 20-1, 30
Whitehall Court 20-1, 53
Windmill Theatre 89